Teapots

Teapots

Makers & Collectors

Dona Z. Meilach

Schiffer Publishing Ltd

4880 Lower Valley Road, Atglen, PA 19310 USA

Dedicated to:
Gloria and Sonny Kamm
for their passion for teapots and admiration of the artists who create them

Frontispiece: Marilyn da Silva, **Harlequin**. (One of a pair.) Copper, brass, gold-plate, gesso, and colored pencil. 4" high, 6" wide, 3" deep. *Courtesy, Mobilia Gallery. Photo, Almac*

Title page: Lazslo Fekete, **Resurrection of a Broken Teapot**. Porcelian and stoneware. (Detail.) 27" high, 12" wide. *Collection, Gloria and Sonny Kamm. Courtesy, Garth Clark Gallery*

Endsheets: Marilyn da Silva, **An Unlikely Pair**. 1998. Copper, brass, gold plate, gesso, and colored pencil. 4" high, 6" wide, 3" deep. *Photo, M. Lee Fatherree*

Library of Congress Cataloging-in-Publication Data:

Meilach, Dona Z.
  Teapots : makers & collectors / by Dona Z. Meilach.
    p. cm.
  ISBN 0-7643-2214-1 (hardcover)
1. Teapots—United States. I. Title.
  NK8730.M45 2005
  642'.7—dc22

                    2005005585

Layout and Cover design by Dona Z. Meilach
Type set in Van Dijk/Souvenir Lt BT

ISBN: 0-7643-2214-1
Printed in China

Published by Schiffer Publishing Ltd.
4880 Lower Valley Road
Atglen, PA 19310
Phone: (610) 593-1777; Fax: (610) 593-2002
E-mail: Info@schifferbooks.com
For the largest selection of fine reference books on this and related subjects,
please visit our web site catalog at **www.schifferbooks.com**
We are always looking for people to write books on new and related subjects. If you have an idea for a book, please contact us at the above address.

This book may be purchased from the publisher.
Include $3.95 for shipping. Please try your bookstore first.
You may write for a free catalog.

In Europe, Schiffer books are distributed by
Bushwood Books
6 Marksbury Ave. Kew Gardens
Surrey TW9 4JF England
Phone: 44 (0)20 8392-8585; Fax: 44 (0)20 8392-9876
E-mail: info@Bushwoodbooks.co.uk
Free postage in the UK. Europe: air mail at cost.
Please try your bookstore first.

Acknowledgments

My sincere thanks and admiration go to Gloria and Sonny Kamm for their cooperation in making this book a reality. They loaned photos from their vast collection of unique teapots and put me in touch with top artists who might have missed my call for entries. They commented on the manuscript offering valuable insight into the world of one-of-a-kind collectible teapots. Their graciousness could not be topped and I am glad that the subject of teapots led to their acquaintance and friendship.

Art gallery directors were generous in their time and effort, and enthusiastic about publicizing this escalating market. Each gallery has a Web site that can be accessed under their name. Upcoming teapot shows are usually listed, along with examples from the shows. My appreciation to:

Adrian Sassoon Gallery, London, England, Clare Beck

Balltimore Clay Works, Baltimore , Maryland

del Mano Gallery, Los Angeles, California, Jan Peters, David Peters, Kirsten Muenster

Garth Glark Gallery, New York, New York, Garth Clark and Masha Portiansky

Habatat Galleries, Royal Oak, Michigan and Chicago, Illinois

Leslie Ferrin Gallery, Lenox, Massachusetts, Leslie Ferrin

Long Beach Museum of Art, Long Beach, California, Harold B. Nelson

Mobilia Gallery, Cambridge, Massachusetts, JoAnn Cooper, Libby Cooper, Anne Hodgsdon

Patina Gallery, Santa Fe, New Mexico, Ivan Barnett, Allison Buchsbaum Barnett

Sherwood Gallery, Inc., Laguna Beach, California, Doris Scruggs

Snyderman/The Works Gallery, Philadelphia, Pennsylvania, Ruth Snyderman

SOFA, Sculptural Objects, Functional Art, Jen Haybach

Yaw Gallery, Birmingham, Michigan; Nancy and Jim Yaw

I am grateful to directors of the many publications and organizations who announced my needs in their pages, Web sites, and bulletin boards.

The photo demonstrations that Christie Beniston and Garry Cohen performed in front of my camera were fun to photograph. Oh, how I appreciated their organization in setting up the procedures. Others who sent me progressive photos of techniques are: Harriete Estel Berman, Frank James Fisher, Sandy and Robert Kinzie, Andi Moran, Faraday Newsome and Jeff Reich, Rollie Younger, Jon Route, Steven Salisian, and Nate Sonnenberg. Thank you, all.

My faithful helper, Sue Kaye of Carlsbad, California, is always available when I most need her impeccable taste, art background, and willingness to help sort and organize photos. Susan Seligman of Albuquerque, New Mexico, shared her information on the tea drinking paraphernalia in Brazil.

I was delighted to tap the expertise and experience of ceramist Erik Gronborg of Solana Beach, California, for his advice on selecting images and checking information in the ceramics chapters. Seymour Zweigoron of Greenville, South Carolina, was fastidious in editing the manuscript. My appreciation goes to Allen Meilach and Shelley Lipman of Los Angeles, California, for discovering artists and galleries as they made their art forays, almost tackling one artist as he rode away from a show on his bicycle.

Without all the excellent photographers, there would be no pictures. I bow in gratitude and admiration to all whose art magic is done behind the lens of a camera. I must acknowledge the tender, loving care of my editors, Nancy and Peter Schiffer, and their staff, for bringing life to the project.

Finally, but primarily, only with the encouragement, help, and patience of my husband, Dr. Melvin Meilach, was I be able to spend the uncountable hours, days, weeks, and months required on the road and in front of the computer to contact, photograph, develop, and write this book.

Carlsbad, California

April, 2005

Preface

When I began collecting material for this book, I wasn't prepared for the overwhelming response and the numbers of people involved in collecting and making teapots. I knew teapot collectors who were in the "minor league" compared to those to whom the teapot hunt is an all-abiding passion. Most collectors were focused on teapots of a specific period, a certain type, or by a certain manufacturer. Many sent photos of their collections that occupied a shelf or two, or the top of a buffet. But those collections didn't intrigue me.

My previous books deal with three dimensional contemporary sculpture so that a collection of traditional Victorian teapots, antique Chinese porcelain, or twentieth century Meissen teapots, while valuable and beautiful, were not the angle I wanted to explore. I needed to find "sculpture" and "contemporary." I didn't want to tread where many others had gone before in scores of books detailing specific types of collectibles.

I let the word out to Web sites, art galleries, and ceramic, silver, and fiber guilds. I sent notices to magazines whose readers might be involved in creating imaginative teapots in materials that could never hold a drop of water.

I had two inspirational yardsticks: Leslie Ferrin and Garth Clark had written wonderful books on contemporary teapots. Both owned art galleries that sold and promoted today's teapot artists. I had been fascinated by the teapot exhibits at the del Mano Gallery in Los Angeles, California, and a few teapot shows in La Jolla, California.

The exhibit that sparked the "book" light in my head was *The Artful Teapot*, that I first viewed at the Long Beach Museum of Art in Long Beach, California, in 2003. It consisted of 250 teapots from the collection of Gloria and Sonny Kamm. Only a small number of their 6000 plus teapots were shown at that time. On display were teapots of every material imaginable, some by artists whose work I had shown in my books on metalwork, woodwork, and fibers. These teapots were awesome, outrageous, fanciful, elegant, exotic, humorous, even erotic, and mind-blowing. This was my cup of tea.

Yes, it was the sculptural and unique teapot that I was after. No matter if it was functional or non-functional. That is what I received from over 400 artists in 14 countries. But I wanted more. I wanted people to understand what went into creating the teapots. How is a ceramic teapot built? How does a flat sheet of silver or pewter become a three dimensional teapot? How does the woodworker turn a piece of a tree trunk or a block of wood into a teapot? How does the glass blower go beyond a vessel form and add a spout, a handle, and a lid to grow a teapot?

When you look at the examples in this book, ooh-ing and aah-ing may be enough. But understanding how they came to be will give you a depth of knowledge that you can carry over into every art form.

I hope that you will turn the pages of this book many, many times and keep it where others, too, can learn to appreciate a form that has gone beyond tradition, and the people who have and continue to take it to who knows where? Please enjoy the fruits of my search as much as I enjoyed the exhilaration of the hunt.

Contents

Opposite page: Ron Korczynski, **Breasty**. Painted and glazed ceramics. 12" high, 12" wide, 9" deep. *Photo, artist*
Right: Bonnie Seeman, **Teapot, 2004**. Porcelain and glass. 8" high. *Courtesy, artist*

Chapter 1
Why Teapots?

The Greeks didn't have them. The Romans didn't have them. Neither did the Minoans or Egyptians. You won't find teapots among the archeological vessels of any of these early "advanced" cultures. Teapots didn't exist before the 1500s, though tea had been a popular drink for centuries before then. Why did it take so long for people to brew tea in pots?

China

The answer is "taxes," the same kind of levies that bring about change in many societies. Yes. During the Cheng-te period of the Ming Dynasty (1368-1644) the marketing and production method for transporting tea was in brick form. Around 1510, when a tax was abolished, tea brick production was discouraged. The option was brewing tea leaves in a bowl. It is amazing that lifting taxation from tea bricks was responsible for the birth of the teapot.

Tea bricks? Yes again. Not tea bags, not instant tea (they came much later). The events that led up to the development of the first teapots by a monk, are fascinating. You can confound your friends with your knowledge of tea lore and heighten your enjoyment of creating or collecting teapots.

First, there had to be tea. One historical version is that we owe the flavorful drink to the Chinese emperor Shen Nung, the father of agriculture and herbal medicine, who lived almost three thousand years before Christ. Allegedly, while working in his garden, he noticed the leaf of a camellia-like bush floating in his bowl of steaming hot water. He took a sip and liked what he tasted. He passed the information around. It spread everywhere even without the aid of E-mail. Over the next centuries of tea cultivation, processing, and marketing, Shen Nung's refreshing and exhilarating drink became an international delight. That's legend, of course, but it makes a good story…and there are others.

Tea appeared in the writing of the Chinese poet Lu Yu in the 8th century and provided a definitive commentary on tea, *Ch'a Ching*, or *The Classic of*

Above:
Turkish women pluck, sort, carry, and process tea leaves. Some plantations use mechanical pluckers but they are not as selective as hand plucking. *Photo, Dona Meilach*

Opposite page:
Tea Plantation, Amaysa, Turkey. Tea is grown in many countries other than China. They include India, Kenya, Sri Lanka (formerly Ceylon), South Asia, South East Asia, and particularly Indonesia, ex-U.S.S.R, Iran, and nine other countries in Africa. There is a growing market in Argentina. Many nations are expanding their tea producing acreage to meet the rising world demand for the most popular beverage. *Photo, Dona Meilach*

Tea, which is still read today. During the T'ang Dynasty (A.D. 618-906) tea was a flavorful and valuable commodity imported to Japan by monks returning from pilgrimages in China. Then tea was shaped into easily transportable bricks. People cut off a chunk of the leaves, crumbled them or pressed them into a powder, then put them into a bowl of boiling water (instant tea?), swished them around and the residue fell to the bottom.

The tea culture permeated China and Japan during the Sung dynasty (A.D. 960-1280). Powdered tea evolved and China developed delicate porcelain tea bowls and teacups, which kept the tea hot. The porcelain industry grew in the city of Jingdezhen, but no teapots were made…only tea bowls and teacups. Teapots and tea sets from Jingdezhen appeared about the mid-1750s. They were exported to other countries in ships laden with tea cargoes, to meet the huge and growing demand for tea in the West.

Japan

The Japanese version of the origin of tea drinking is credited to the missionary monk, Daruma (Prince Bodhidharma), who brought Buddhism from India to China and Japan. In A.D. 520, he began a nine-year meditation in a cave-temple near Canton. Understandably, he fell asleep after months of staring at a stone wall. Unhappy that he dozed during this meditation, he cut off his betraying eyelids and threw them to the ground. The resulting tea plant that grew provided Daruma with an elixir that kept him alert during the remaining years of his meditation.

The Japanese tea ceremony, *Chanoyu*, began about the 9th century. Over the next few hundred years, and until the 12th century, tea drinking, along with other emerging rituals, languished during the social, political, and cultural disarray of Kublai Khan and the Mongols. Later, during the Ming dynasty (A.D. 1368-1644) many of the lost rituals were revived. Tea plantations appeared, methods for processing tea emerged and the black, green, and oolong teas we know today were developed. Still people retrieved the essence of tea leaves in a bowl. The leaves had to be swished about with a tea whisk and strained, or left in the bottom of the bowl.

The First Teapots

Between A.D. 1506 and1521, during the Ming dynasty in China, it is believed that a monk began forming a vessel from the purple clay found abundantly in the hills around Yixing (pronounced ee-shing) located about 150 kilometers from Shanghai. He worked the clumps of clay into a teapot and, in time, Yixing became the teapot pottery center. The fine-grained, colorful purple and red clays were so satiny and beautiful that no glazes were used. Today, we know that these small teapots had an indelible influ-

A tea vendor in Amaysa, Turkey, carries a large brass teapot on his back. The pouring spout fits under his arm, teacups are stored in his belt. To serve a customer, the vendor removes a cup from his belt, bends at the waist, the tea spout lowers, and tea pours into the cup he holds in his hand. *Photo, Dona Meilach*

ence on ceramic design that spread to Japan, Korea, Thailand, and throughout Europe. Eventually, art historians dubbed this style of decorative arts in the West as "Chinoiserie," indicating designs based on Chinese influences.

As Yixing pottery production emerged, individual potters were recognized. They signed their pots, as opposed to anonymous artisans who created vessels for mass production. An artist-pottery movement grew. It included scholars who examined the teapot's design and debated its ideal proportions: A wide bottom enhances stability. A spout high on the pot lets you fill it to the brim. A snug lid helps retain heat, and it should be planned so it doesn't fall out when the pot is tilted. The opening should accommodate the infusion basket that holds the leaves. It should be big enough so a sponge or brush can be inserted for cleaning. Finally, a handle should be comfortable to grip and make pouring easy.

How Tea Is Grown And Processed

Almost all tea leaves are plucked from the *camellia sinensis* plant. The process by which the different teas are made depends on the fermentation used. It differs for white tea, green tea, oolong, and black tea. Tea, much like grapes for wine, will differ by where the plants are grown, the climate, and the altitude.

The evergreen tea bush, or shrub, favors a humid, jungle like environment. The best teas grow above 5000 feet where the harsher conditions are conducive to the plants slower development and maturity. The leaves are selectively plucked from the bush. Plucking tea leaves can be done by motorized equipment, but mechanical plucking cannot discern which leaves to select. In many countries, leaves are still plucked by women who select top leaves, central leaves, or shoots. Different leaves yield different qualities of tea. Top leaves produce a harsher, stronger brew than leaves plucked from young shoots. An experienced tea leaf plucker can pick enough leaves in one day to produce nine pounds of finished tea, equal to eighteen hundred cups of tea. That amounts to the estimated number of cups one British tea drinker will consume in a year.

Teapots Traverse The Oceans

As shipments of tea included Jingdezhen porcelain and Yixing clay teapots they had a significant influence around the world. Drinking tea became fashionable and gave rise to the British "high tea". It also gave rise to pottery centers that developed in Britain around the end of the 18th century.

The new British potteries soon manufactured copies of Chinese teapots plus new designs. Their teapots and tea sets were cleverly marketed to create a demand. For instance, tea services were deemed a fashionable acces-

Hongshen Zhao, **Mythical Animal Teapot**. Purple Yixing clay. The contrasting insets are also of Yixing local clay that is natural in 3 colors. Some clay is stained for additional colors and involves a long, time-consuming process. 3.5" high, 6" wide. *Photo, Sandy Kinzie*

Zhou Guangzhen Zho and Mei-Qun-Gu, **Shifted No. 5**. 2003. Many artists emulate Yixing style teapots or make their own modern versions based on the Yixing style. Yixing pots typically are unglazed so have a matte finish. 6.6" high, 4.7" wide, 4.3" deep. *Photo, artists*

11

sory with new designs appearing regularly. Hostesses felt they had to have the latest tea service when they entertained.

By the mid-1750s, novelty teapots appeared in the shapes of pineapples, cauliflowers, and various exotic fruits. Almost any object that could be visualized as a teapot was made, including two-story houses, birds, dragons, large animals, celebrities, and public political figures. Imaginations ran wild. Inventive potters produced teapots tht were humorous and serious, and sold by the thousands. Today, for example, cockerels, monkeys, animals, and fish shapes, produced in the 19th Century by the Staffordshire firms of Minton, and George Jones in Majolica, are now rare, expensive, and sought after.

Arts & Crafts Movement

In the late 1800s and early 1900s, new concepts for ceramics and teapots appeared, based on the growing influence of the Arts & Crafts movement in Great Britain. The writings of William Morris were put into practice by artists such as René Lalique (glass), Christopher Dresser (silver), and Victor Horta, (ironwork). They extolled the concept of individualized objects made by craftspeople in their studios. For ceramists, the term "studio potter" was applied and is still used.

A special exhibition, *The Stonewares of Charles Fergus Binns: The Father of American Studio Ceramics,* was held in 1998 at Alfred University. It featured approximately 110 stoneware vases, jars, bottles, and bowls Binns created between 1905 and 1934, while teaching at Alfred University in New York state. Binns is often referred to as the "Father of American studio ceramics." This title reflects his unique stoneware pots in the Arts & Crafts style, and also acknowledges vital information about ceramic clay bodies and glaze recipes he developed. An important legacy he left was a book, titled *The Potter's Craft,* that has been reprinted three times since the first 1910 edition.

Another impetus came in 1900 with New York Governor Teddy Roosevelt's bill establishing the New York State School of Clay-Working and Ceramics (now the New York State College of Ceramics at Alfred University). Binns was appointed the founding Director and held the position for more than thirty years until his retirement in 1931.

In the post-World War II era, young artists were flocking to colleges where they enrolled in expanding art programs. The American Crafts Council evolved along with magazines reporting on crafts activities and who was doing what.

Rough textured small Japanese ceramic teapots are used in a traditional Japanese Tea Ceremony. The left one is only 5" high and holds 5 ounces; the smaller one is 4" high and holds 3 ounces. They are ample for cups used in the tea ceremony. A tea whisk, used when stirring tea in a tea bowl, is shown at the rear. *Meilach collection. Photo, Dona Meilach*

Teapots in an assembly line ready for painting and firing. Though the shapes are repetitious, the decorations differ so that no two are exactly alike. Often, painting is done "piece-meal." Each worker may paint the portions at which he or she is an expert; one does eyes, another does mouths, and so forth. *Photo, Dona Meilach*

The teapot is the king of the items used for tea, other accessories are cups and saucers, tea balls, tea strainers, tea bag squeezers, teaspoons, and hundreds of types of tea sold loosely and in tea bags. Additionally, there are traditional foods served with tea such as scones, tea cakes, tea sandwiches, biscotti, and cookies. In 1904 Thomas Sullivan, a New York food merchant economized by sending his merchants tea samples in small silk bags rather than tins. This was quickly recognized as a good method for brewing tea. *Photo, Dona Meilach*

In Brazil's Pantanal, cowboys drink Yerba Maté tea, known as tereré, from a cow horn. The cow horn's bottom hole is plugged with a wood peg. Tea leaves are placed in the horn bottom, and hot water is added. They drink it through a filter straw, called a bombilla, (bom-bee-ya). The "tereré" is passed around in a group, adding water to the horn, often directly from the river. This cow horn is 5" high, 2.5" diam. The filter/straw, made of a rust-proof alloy of zinc, magnesium, and iron, is 7.5" long. *Collection, Susan Seligman. Photo, Dona Meilach*

The New Influences

In the early 1960s, First Lady of the United States Jacqueline Kennedy had spearheaded a movement to encourage arts and crafts by instituting a White House craft collection. Most of the artists whose work is in that collection went on to become nationally recognized artists with wonderful reputations. After Mrs. Kennedy's husband's assassination, Lady Bird Johnson, the new First Lady, picked up the torch and continued to promote crafts in America.

By the 1970s new enthusiasm for one-of-a-kind teapots by artists gripped the crafts communities and collectors jumped into the arena. Senator Walter F. Mondale served as the American Ambassador to Japan in the 1970s. While living in Tokyo, he and his wife, Joan Mondale, took a leadership role in the national crafts movement that was bubbling in America. They used their official residence as a showcase for the work of contemporary American craft artists. Every year, Mrs. Mondale mounted a major exhibition of paintings, sculpture, and crafts from across America. Later, back in the United States when her husband served as Vice President under Jimmy Carter, Mrs. Mondale, herself an accomplished potter, continued to take an active role in promoting American crafts.

The Washington Post reported that Mrs. Mondale bought, with her own household money, a 16-place luncheon service of pottery... hand-blown goblets... glass dessert plates...placemats... and salt and pepper shakers. She also commissioned a rocking chair to be made by Sam Maloof.

Artists working in clay began making serious and novelty teapots. They were taking a cue from the small potteries in England that were turning out functional novelty teapots by the thousands that people were gleefully collecting. The English potteries labeled their pieces hand-painted, so they were deemed one-of-kind. In truth, the decorations were often done assembly-line fashion with one person drawing all the eyes, another doing hair, another the clothing, and so forth. Several potteries manufactured certain designs as "limited editions" so that the prices would escalate as editions sold out, thereby making them more valuable to collectors.

Studio potters continued to produce teapots that were functional, traditional, and often, novel. By the 1990s the functional teapot had already given way to the "sculptural teapot," and function was not a prime requirement. The teapot form was embraced as a design challenge by artists in

Inset at left:
Guayakí handcrafted pre-Columbian design gourd and a bombilla are also used for drinking Yerba Maté. *Courtesy, Guayakí Sustainable Rainforest Products*

13

many media. Ceramic pots dominated, because of the ease with which clay could be manipulated. Silversmiths, too, began digressing from the formality of English tea services with new forms, though they remained functional as well as sculptural. Artistic, sculptural teapots now appeared in various metals, wood, glass, fibers, and found objects, as well as ceramics.

Garth Clark's book *The Eccentric Teapot* (1989) first sparked awareness of artistic teapots. Leslie Ferrin, a ceramist, had opened a gallery called "The Pinch Pottery" in 1979, in Massachusetts, that became her Leslie Ferrin Gallery in 1987, showing and selling innovative teapots to a small coterie of collectors. Her book, *Teapots Transformed* (2000), gave additional credibility to the movement and it's been an uphill course since then. You will find these "transformed" teapots throughout this book. Whether you're a maker or a collector, or just an interested observer, the examples shown will open a new appreciation of this exciting art form.

News Note

If there is any doubt about the value of early Chinese pots, a news item in 2004 reported thefts of priceless porcelain vessels from a government storage facility in Jingdezhen. The thieves tunneled into the old and ancient kilns, despite their being protected properties designated by the government of China as historical sites. The porcelain pieces stored in the kilns included vases, teapots, and other pottery pieces. They were Kuan pieces, meaning pieces that were owned by the imperial family.

An estimation of the value of these pieces was established in 1999, when one vase was sold at an auction in Hong Kong for HK $30,000,000. The stolen pottery pieces value amounted to up to 10 times the number of pieces in the museum.

This purloined kiln, discovered in early 2000, was 10 feet deep. Thieves managed to get into the storeroom via a wooden walkway that was tunneled into a mountain. The previous year authorities had managed to catch a thief while he was tunneling. There were at least 50 such cases in the previous two years. The 2004 theft was a very painful lesson for the authorities.

When people think of teapots, the most likely image is of fine bone china or porcelain ware such as Delft teapots from Holland, or Limoges, Chelsea, and Staffordshire China from England. Here, a Chinese teapot waits for a collector to find it in a Los Angeles, California antique shop. *Photo, Dona Meilach*

Marek Cecula, **Mutant II**. 1998. Porcelain on a wood base. White chinaware is associated with teapots from China or England. Today's potters may be inspired by traditional forms, but then design teapots in a modern idiom. Teapot: 12" high, 12" wide. *Courtesy, Garth Clark Gallery, New York, New York*

Christopher Dresser, **Untitled Tea Set**. 1903. Sterling silver with a rattan handle. During the Arts &
Crafts movement in the early 1900s, and the emergence of Art Nouveau, Christopher Dresser's
(1834-1904) simple tea service was in direct contrast to the highly ornate Victorian, and earlier, silver
hollowware produced in England. *Collection, Gloria and Sonny Kamm. Photo, Tony Cunha*

Annette Corcoran, **Scarlet Tanager**. 2003. Porcelain. The artist has been interested in both birds and teapots for about 20 years. Those who collect only teapots with birds will invariably have one of Corcoran's hand painted teapots in their collection. 10.5" high, 8" wide, 5.5" deep. *Leslie Ferrin Gallery, Lenox, Massachusetts. Photo, Patrick Tregenza*

Left:
Jerry Rothman, **Ritual Vessel Teapot**. 1970. In the 1960s, ceramic artists had expanded the boundaries of traditional ceramic styles. In time, the teapot became a sculptural expressive object. Rothman experimented with new clays, shapes, glazes, and even new sizes, for a series of vessels he made based on historical art styles. *Courtesy, artist.*

Gina Freuen, **Slope Foot Teapot with Teapot Companion**. Porcelain with varied textures and glazes. A small teapot becomes the top for the larger one. Many ceramists now use fine porcelain for an incredible variety of teapot shapes with unique textures and concepts. 12" high, 14" wide, 3" deep. *Photo, artist*

Candace Kling, **Pot du Choclat Blanc**. 2002. Acetate satin fabric, nylon thread, copper rod, lightweight buckram, and glues. Techniques include molding, folding, pressing, stitching, and gluing. The piece was developed as a challenge for combining shape and textures reminiscent of white chocolate or of ruffles on a Victorian gown. 5" high, 15" wide, 7" deep. *Collection, Myra Goodall Block. Courtesy, Mobilia Gallery, Cambridge, Massachusetts. Photo, John Bagley*

Jack da Silva, **Esteemed Tea: Self-Help II**. Sterling silver spigot, glass head quilter pins, and many corks. When a non-functional teapot is to be created, the artist can become as inventive and fanciful as his imagination and materials will allow. 6" high, 4" wide, 5" deep. *Photo, M. Lee Fatherree*

Teapots are Pervasive In Today's Society

In 2003, at the Long Beach Museum of Art in Long Beach, California, the museum exhibit, *The Artful Teapot*, enjoyed an unprecedented number of visitors. An oversized Fiberglas teapot on the museum's grounds set the stage for the show. Outside the museum, a huge inflated balloon teapot called attention to the exhibit.

The Artful Teapot exhibit showcased 250 of the over 6000 (and growing) teapot collection of Gloria and Sonny Kamm. This collection also includes a teapot playhouse the Kamms purchased for their grandchildren at a Home Aid Charity auction. There is also a teapot that had been used in the Disneyland Main Street Parades. The exhibit had previously appeared at the Copia Museum in Napa, California. Additional venues were in Chicago, Illinois; Toronto, Canada; Charlotte, North Carolina; Montgomery, Alabama; and other cities in America. A future teapot museum is being planned in Sparta, North Carolina, as a catalyst to draw visitors to the area for economic revitalization.

Often, a teapot is used as signage for tea shops. Kate Malone's clock teapot hangs above a store in a shopping mall in England. For another installation, a large teapot was commissioned. She always makes two of a commissioned piece, should some disaster befall one of them during the drying, firing, shipping, or other procedures along the way. Malone's "back-up" teapot is on exhibit at a British museum.

Commercially made new teapots can be found in department store housewares sections, gift shops, tourist shops, galleries, museum stores…almost everywhere. Older teapots can be found in antique shops, flea markets, yard sales, estate sales, and resale shops. One only has to look to appreciate how pervasive they have become in our lives.

The idea of having the teapot steam *every* hour to remind people to come to drink tea sounds simple. However, the engineering was complicated and turned into a major challenge because of the center's fire regulations. Final engineering resulted in the steam being produced in a sealed unit on the roof. It takes the steam seven seconds to travel down through a tube, through columns, through the point of attachment inside the clock face, then up and out through the spout. The clock required seven men 14 hours to assemble and install on site.

A huge Fiberglas teapot accompanied the exhibit *The Artful Teapot*, at the Long Beach Museum of Art, Long Beach, California, in 2003. The exhibit displayed 250 varied teapots from the Gloria and Sonny Kamm collection. *Photo, Dona Meilach*

Kate Malone, **Time for Tea.** 1998. 9 ft. wide. Clock for Bentalls Centre, Kingston upon Thames. Stoneware clay and crystalline glazed, coil built by hand over a steel and aluminum body. The hour markers were made with the assistance of Yola Spytkowska. The clock is double sided with an exaggerated spout, lid, and handle for dramatic effect, as it is 40 feet up in the air. The clock, based on a traditional "Brown Betty" English teapot, emits steam every hour on the hour. *Photo, courtesy artist*

Kate Malone. **Teapot.** Malone always makes a second clock when she has a large commission should a disaster occur with the first one during firing, delivery, or installation. This extra teapot is on display at a Norwich, England museum.

19

Jerry Rothman, **Archaic Ritual Vessel**. 1977. Ceramic. Teapots by internationally known artists that were created several years ago have collectible value. For such pieces, it is easy to learn about the artist and why a particular piece is significant. 18" high, 18" wide, 7" diam. *Collection, Gloria & Sonny Kamm. Courtesy, artist*

Chapter 2
Makers and Collectors

What is there about teapots that is so appealing? There are almost as many answers as there people who collect them. Socializing and nostalgia harkening back to parents' and grandparents' homes, are often cited. Collecting provides an object to "search for" when people travel, something a family can seek out together. When displayed, teapots generate comments and conversation. They are pleasant to look at and enjoy, and they make people happy.

Most mass produced functional teapots are attractive, colorful, varied, and affordable. But how many functional teapots can a person use? Extras are displayed on kitchen counters, on buffets, in china cabinets, and on specially built shelving. When three or four teapots are gathered, one becomes a "collector" without realizing it.

In time, these collectors focus their tastes, and become selective in the pieces they seek. One couple buys on the basis of materials used; perhaps porcelain, stoneware, Majolica, terra-cotta, or a painted style. Another collector seeks teapots with birds. Someone else looks for humorous teapots. Still others concentrate on teapots that have landscapes, tell a story, represent celebrities, are abstract, or geometric. Some collectors will opt for the work of two or three artists; others will collect as many artists as possible.

The confirmed collector begins to go beyond what he or she can find in gift shops, flea markets, and resale shops. Prices for teapots increase and, in time, their value to other collectors may increase just as it does if one were investing in paintings or sculptures by well known artists.

The next step up sends them searching for one-of-a-kind teapots. The search may be confined; perhaps to ones that are whimsical, architectural, or with specific subjects. In their hunt for "something different", the goal may be elusive until they spot *that* teapot that is *exactly* what they had in mind.

An idea for a teapot may exist in a collector's mind's eye, and a growing number of artists are catering to these eclectic and discerning tastes. The collectors now seek their elusive style teapots at up-scale craft fairs, art galleries, and auctions. They may buy directly from the artist and, if they can recognize

Nate Sonnenberg, **Desert # 4**. 2004. Sandblasted ceramic with a metal handle. The simplicity of this teapot belies the research and artisanship involved. Sonnenberg uses the Yixing concepts to create a series of pots with clay he colors to simulate Yixing clay. 8" high, 6" wide, 4" deep. *Photo, Michael Cavanaugh*

an up and coming talent whose work they admire, they may commission an artist to create a teapot. They hope that other collectors will corroborate their taste and the teapot's value will increase as the artist's reputation escalates.

With more gallery owners recognizing their customers' escalating romance with teapots, they are mounting teapot exhibitions and fanning the collectible trend. They encourage the artists they represent to try their hand at teapots and, generally, the pieces walk off the gallery pedestals. The result is an astonishing and provoking array of teapots in various media that may challenge the viewer to find a hidden spout or handle. The teapots can be fanciful, elegant, abstract, organic, figurative, exotic, and satirical. At the same time the artists use the teapot form to explore color, form, and content in exceptional ways.

Suzanne Maxwell creates myriad geometric shapes and then assembles them into unique teapots. *Courtesy artist*

A potter's wheel in the hands of Nate Sonnenberg is as natural as a dish on a dinner table. *Photo, Zeal C. Estrada*

Garry Cohen creates colorful glass teapots using traditional glass blowing techniques.

Booths displaying one-of-kind teapots are often found at craft fairs. Barry Hage tends the booth with pots by Rosalind and Barry Hage. *Photo, Rosalind Hage*

Binh Pho made a teapot for a special gallery exhibition and found they were a welcome addition to the intricately carved and embellished lathe turned wood vessels for which he is well known. *Courtesy, artist*

Who and Where are the Teapot Artists?

Artists who create unique teapots for today's collector's are from small towns and big cities. They work from home studios, corners of garages, in art cooperatives, and school art departments. Many teach and work at colleges and universities, sharing their knowledge and passion for creativity to talented, motivated students. Current college students are unhampered by tradition and are free to let their imaginations soar. And they do. Several examples in the book are by graduate level arts students and their pieces fare very well next to those by established artists with excellent credentials, reputations, and gallery representation.

The artists create in many media: clay, metal, glass, wood, fibers, and more. Each has an individual approach and philosophy. Their work can be seen in studios, at craft fairs, in gift shops, and galleries worldwide. Artists who submitted work for this book represent fourteen countries including Australia, Austria, Canada, China, England, Finland, France, Germany, Ireland, Japan, Scotland, Switzerland, Taiwan, and the United States.

Clay teapots outnumber those in other media, so this chapter and chapters 3 and 4 focus on the techniques for creating ceramic teapots. In the following chapters, you will discover artists who work in silver, mixed metals, glass, wood, fibers and beads, and combinations of materials. They use a boggling number of techniques. Those pictured at left will give you an idea of who they are and how they work; you'll find many others as you delve into each chapter.

Suzanne E. Maxwell from Marlton, New Jersey, strives to create a feeling of movement and spontaneity in her teapots to parallel the excitement she has for life and for working with clay. She throws a variety of geometric clay cylinders, cone, bowl, and doughnut shapes on a potter's wheel. While the clay is still wet, she cuts, bends, and manipulates the thrown sections which may be combined with hand built elements to complete the form. Originally, her vessels were practical for pouring tea, but now the form and ideas are more important. Surfaces are enhanced using pressed textures and layers of stains, underglazes, and low-fired glazes. Her teapots incorporate active organic lines to mimic life and suggest growth.

Nate Sonnenberg is an artist, ceramist, a Kung Fu martial artist, and a teacher in the School of Fine Arts at Indiana University, Bloomington, Indiana. He holds a B.F.A. and an M.A. in ceramics and is working on his third degree, a Master's in Fine Arts in Ceramics. He is also deeply involved studying the Yixing pottery tradition and is creating 100 teapots in the Yixing style exploring new forms and shapes. He is as at home and comfortable at a potter's wheel as he is at a dining room table.

Garry Cohen heads the glass art department at Palomar College, San Marcos, California, and has developed clever, beautifully colored rooster and chicken teapots in blown glass. His demonstration can be seen in Chapter 7.

Teapots in fine china, bone china, and porcelain, are often associated with English or Chinese teapots. Some people collect only pots from one manufacturer, one historical time, or one artistic style. *Photo courtesy, Earl Grey Tea*

Rosalind and Barry Hage, from Long Beach, California, create teapot decorations, colors, and surface treatments inspired by objects seen during their extensive travels. Rosalind, a teacher turned ceramist, joined Barry in his ceramic studio. She brought organization and people skills along with a raw creativity that blended well with Barry's work. Barry is shown at a craft fair standing before a booth exhibiting their ceramics.

Binh Pho's lathe-turned, pierced, carved, and intricately decorated wood vessels with Chinese imagery are collected widely. He uses wood as a symbol of living things, and the negative spaces represent the unseen weight of the unknown. Originally from Vietnam, he now works from a studio in Maple Park, Illinois, a suburb west of Chicago, Illinois.

Traditional Teapots

Some people confine their collecting to traditional pots. They might be old English or Chinese porcelain, or pots from Yixing. They might concentrate on teapots from specific designers or manufacturers. Many of today's ceramists continue to produce pots that are more traditional and functional than those illustrated and these appeal to many tastes.

Wedgwood pots have always been a favorite collectible. In May 1759, Josiah Wedgwood (1730-1795) left Thomas Whieldon's workshop and established himself as an independent potter. He was twenty-eight, ambitious, and eager to test his talents. His new establishment at Burslem, England, consisted of a cottage, two kilns, sheds, and workrooms, all rented from his cousin, John Wedgwood, for £15 a year (about $1,350 US dollars today).

For the next three years, Josiah, his cousin Thomas, and several hired hands manufactured tortoiseshell and other ware. Josiah began coating creamware in new brilliant glazes he had perfected while working with Whieldon. He also purchased ornate molds representing pineapples, cauliflowers, cabbages, and pears. Using good marketing skills, the Wedgwood name became famous, and still is, more than 200 years later.

Cardew Designs of Devon, in Southern England, a well-known china company, produces limited editions of unique collectible pots that reflect peoples' current interests. They introduce teapots representing current popular movies, new and old cartoon characters, such as the *Betty Boop* teapot shown, *Spiderman*, and Mickey Mouse as *The Sorcerer's Apprentice*.

Intrepid collectors search for teapots from certain china companies such as Russell Wright, Hall China, Fitz and Floyd, three American companies whose teapot designs border on the modern. These companies, and their teapot designs, can be seen on their Web sites and at resale and auction Web sites such as eBay.

Institutional Collectors

With the popularity of teapots expanding, many museum curators are amassing teapots from the growing ranks of talented artists. Almost every artist who submitted photos for this book listed collectors in their resumes. These included museums in many countries, universities, banks, hospitals, and large corporations. Curators recognize that today's non-functional teapots are sculptures as pure and straightforward as an abstract monolith, a bronze figure, or a man on a horse.

The Bramah Teapot Museum, two minutes from London Bridge Station, in London, England, is the world's first museum devoted entirely to the history of tea and coffee. It tells the commercial and social 400-year-old history of two of the world's most important commodities since their arrival in Europe from the Far East and Africa. The British played a major role in the China trade and tea production in India, Ceylon, and Africa, so the museum, as one might expect, tells the story from a British perspective. The museum, through its ceramics, metalware, prints, and displays, answers all the questions that people from around the world ask about British tea and coffee.

Wedgwood is a type of pottery made by Josiah Wedgwood (1730-1795) and his successors. Typically, they have a classical decoration in white on a blue background. Wedgwood teapots are among many British made teapots favored by collectors for their antiquity, historical value, and appeal. 12" high. *Private collection. Photo, Dona Meilach*

Betty Boop, From the Cardew Design Company in Devon, England. Cardew introduces new designs regularly in limited editions that quickly become sought after by collectors. 5" high. *Private collection*

The Pinglin Tea Industry in Taiwan built what is purportedly the world's largest museum devoted to tea. Opened on January 12, 1997, it is located in the green hills of Pinglin in Taipei County, overlooking a picturesque waterway. It took eight years and US $10 million to complete and features a pleasant Chinese style garden where oolong tea is served to all visitors.

Celestial Seasonings Tea Company maintains a teapot collection. Through the years they have held contests for artist-made teapots and the wining teapots are on display at their headquarters store near Boulder, Colorado. Tours of their Art Gallery are available where one can also view original paintings from their tea boxes created by some of the country's most famous illustrators.

Lipton Tea sponsored a teapot competition in 2004 with the winners' teapots displayed and sold through a gallery in Scottsdale, Arizona.

The teapot collection of Gloria and Sonny Kamm is circulating to art museums around the country. It displays 250 examples of incredibly different teapots from their more than 6000 teapot collection. The book by Garth Clark, *The Eccentric Teapot*, provides a first overview of unique teapots. *The Artful Teapot*, based on the pieces in the Kamm exhibition, helps people understand that teapots were, indeed, taking a new artistic direction. Their collection will be permanently housed in the Sparta Teapot Museum in Sparta, North Carolina, in 2008 and can be previewed at www.spartateapotmuseum.org. *Teapots Transformed*, by Leslie Ferrin, emphasized the idea that teapots can be collected and enjoyed. Both Garth Clark (New York, New York) and Leslie Ferrin (Lenox, Massachusetts) have galleries that specialize in teapots. Galleries, such as del Mano in Los Angeles, California, and Mobilia Gallery in Cambridge, Massachusetts, and many others, mount annual teapot exhibits. Pieces from the shows can be viewed on each gallery's Web site.

The Racine Art Museum, Racine, Wisconsin, was gifted the clay teapot collection (over 250 teapots) of Donna Moog, spanning the years 1980 to the late 1990s. The museum has produced a book with the images titled, *Tea, Anyone?* The forward, written by Peter Shire notes: "Themes common in contemporary art of the period focus on the figure, personal narrative, and the role of women in today's society."

Teapot collecting is a generations old activity in England. In 1998, Linda and Vince McDonald launched the "Totally Teapots" club for collectors of whimsical teapots initially because that was their passion. It can be found at www.totallyteapots.com. Teapot Island is literally a small island off the coast of England in Yalding, near Maidstone, Kent, where Sue Blazye runs a teashop and a museum of over 3,500 teapots. See www.teapotisland.com.

All these displays are stirring up interest and appreciation of today's artist made teapots. Functional, or non-functional, it's an art form that is here to stay.

Rachel Porter, **Tropical Teapot**. Porcelain. People often collect teapots dealing with specific subjects. Fish and marine subjects are favorites, realistic and imaginative. 8" high, 8" wide, 3" deep. *Photo, artist*

Bramah Museum of Tea and Coffee. Within this interesting storefront in London exists this internationally known museum. *Photo courtesy, Edward Bramah*

Bramah Museum of Tea and Coffee. Displaying teapots can be tricky. It's hard to display them where they can be seen from all sides without turning them around. Several one-of-a kind teapots are in the Bramah permanent collection and are not for sale.Tea is also served offering a choice of exotic varieties from different countries. *Photo courtesy, Edward Bramah*

For Ricky Maldonado, clay is his life. All pieces are coil built with terra cotta clay. When dry, he sands and smoothes the surface using the sanded particles to make *terra siggalatta* a thick liquid clay called "slip." He burnishes the piece with his hands or a soft cloth. A portion of the terra siggalatta is colored to contrast with the clay body, and applied with a sable brush, one dot at time, before it is fired. Maldonado is greatly influenced by his Native American heritage. Additionally, details in clothing, architecture, and people that surround him are fodder for his creative mind. The photo shows his work on display at the del Mano Gallery, Los Angeles, California. It also indicates that craft galleries are a prime source for seeing and buying collectible teapots.

A classic example of a valuable and collectible teapot is by Jerry Rothman (page 20) who was active from the 1960s. Rothman created a variety of "Ritual Vessels" in the late 1970s representing different historic art styles: archaic, classic, baroque, and modern. He says, "The vessel form, including teapots, allowed me to break away from traditional constraints and create a uniquely American form that would be applicable in modern American society."

By redirecting the applications for ceramics, Rothman's vessels were historically significant, as well as beautiful, and technically mature. Collectors Gloria and Sonny Kamm purchased two of his early pieces for their growing collection. In an overview of the history of ceramics, the purchase represents the growth and change in ceramic style. The teapots have been exhibited in museums showing the development of Rothman's style as well and his influence on other ceramists of the time.

Yixing teapots, mentioned in Chapter 1, are a favorite of collectors. It's not unusual for an American potter to emulate the Yixing style, as well as the clay. These simulations themselves become collectible because of the expertise of those who make them and the results. Richard Notkin's reputation for Yixing style pots is well established. He uses the clays and finish inherent to

Ricky Maldonado. Large, hand painted ceramic teapots on display at the del Mano Gallery, Los Angeles, California, illustrate unique pots, where to look for them, and ideas for displaying them effectively, *del Mano Gallery. Photo, Dona Meilach*

Walter Reiss, **Dysfunctional Teapots**. 2003. Ceramic collectible teapots can be found at many art-craft fairs throughout the country. Teapot makers find a ready market for them among today's enthusiastic collectors. *Photo, Dona Meilach*

the Yixing pots, but his statements are strictly his own...frequently with political or social overtones.

Another collectible Yixing potter is Nate Sonnenberg who once was a student of Richard Notkin. Both Notkin and Sonnenberg have spent time at the pottery facilities in Yixing, China, and other pottery centers nearby. Sonnenberg mixes his own clay using a high iron content and some manganese to give the clay its dark brown coloring. He likes to leave the clay unglazed to achieve the texture and untreated look of the natural tone of the Yixing clay. Sonnenberg works in two spheres of the Chinese tradition; ceramics and martial arts. He has won world championship titles for his demonstration-performance of a traditional Chinese Kung-Fu Eagle Claw Form.

For collectors, Yixing teapots are like honey to bees. For centuries they have been considered the best vessel for brewing tea. They have been renowned for their unique artistry and practical usage by incorporating the concepts of aesthetic beauty and natural harmony. The stunning Yixing style teapots shown (page 28) were made in Jiangsu province, an area situated 120 miles northwest of Shanghai, China, not far from Yixing.

Yixing pots are small by Western standards. The purple, brown, and red clays used for Yixing earthenware teapots have several unique characteris-

Above:
Zhou Guangzhen Zho and Mei-Qun-Gu, **Generation #1**. 2003. Stoneware. Yixing style. 11.4" high, 18" wide, 18" deep. Photo, artist

Top left:
Zhou Ding Fang, **Bag and Mouse**. 1994. Fang is a well-known contemporary Yixing artist whose teapots have fascinating themes often with bugs and small animals. People may collect pots from one artist, or pots with specific themes. 3.5" high, 8" wide, 2.75" deep. *Photo, artist*

Bottom right:
Sunshine. Not all teapots have to be handmade, costly, and non- functional. This novelty teapot from China cost 99-cents. It is functional, except the glaze wore away quickly. People who buy one or two novelty teapots may become "hooked" into serious collecting. *Photo, Dona Meilach*

Allan Rosenbaum, **Tele-Tea**. 2001. Earthenware, with stains and glazes. The pot encompasses much of the artist's philosophy and makes a social statement within the context of a sculptural teapot. 7" high, 12" wide, 11" deep. *Photo, Katherine Wetzel*

Allan Rosenbaum, **Guidebook Teapot**. Teapots with the shape of an object have been around almost since the beginning of teapot making. There are teapots as stoves, as refrigerators, as baby buggies. This object has humor built in as well. 11.5" high, 12" wide, 5" deep. *Photo, Katherine Wetzel*

tics. The entire contents of each brew can be quickly emptied after each infusion. This assures that the tea is served without the bitterness that may occur when tea leaves are left to steep. With continued usage the porous clay teapots will absorb the aroma and flavors of the tea. Experts suggest that you need only pour water into the pot to taste the brew. They recommend using a different pot for each type of tea. The pots withstand high temperatures and are slow to conduct heat so the handle remains comfortably cool even when pouring very hot tea.

Allan Rosenbaum's *Tele Tea* is in the form of a telephone. He deliberately juxtaposes two common objects with different associations. A teapot is used in a social setting—A telephone offers the possibility or the illusion of intimacy. He says, "In this work I address concerns about the nature of human relationships, our methods of communications, and the importance of community." He hopes people will look at this work as an imaginative transformation of a common object into art.

Joan Irvin, **Noisy Neighbor Teapot**. Low-fire clay and glazes with gold luster. Some collectors seek teapots only of people or of different heads and facial expressions. They may be humorous, celebrities, or caricatures. 6.5" high, 8" long, 6.5" deep. *Photo, artist*

Vipoo Srivlasa, **Deep Sea Spike**. Earthenware color glaze and gold luster. From his Mythical Monster Teapot Series. Press mold, hand-built. 8" high, 6.3" wide, 8" deep. *Photo, artist*

Porntip Sangvanich, **Untitled Teapot**. 2004. Earthenware. Made of assembled clay parts in a frankly non-functional design. It becomes pure sculpture although a teapot form. 12.25" high, 13" wide, 3.5" deep. *Photo, artist*

Dina Angel-Wing, **Tea-Vee Teapot**. Teapots may be tinged with humor, whimsy, and be a pun both visually and verbally. *Photo, Frank Wing*

Meryl H. Ruth, **Tea Clutch**. 2004. Stoneware. Replicas of real objects entice many artists, and collectors may fashion their entire collection around one or more types of such objects. 8" high, 7.5" wide, 4" deep. *Photo, Robert Diamante*

Teapot Purse. Naugahyde. Often, someone designs a purse or other utilitarian objects as a one-of-a-kind and it becomes so desirable that it is put into production. *Photo, Dona Meilach*

Anne Kraus, **Last Chance Hotel**. Ceramic tile. 2002. Some collectors opt for objects that contain teapots, or are teapots in a form other than a 3-dimensional vessel. *Courtesy, Garth Clark Gallery, New York, New York.*

Teapot Brooch. Ceramic pin with chain was made from a mold so multiples could be produced. Each may differ somewhat in color, or surface design, as they are hand painted. *Collection, Dona Meilach. Photo, Don Diehl*

Jerry Berta, **Mr. T-Pot, I Pity The Fool That Don't Buy It**! The life-size sculpture/teapot is a cross between the artist, Mr. T, and a teapot. The head lifts off and is a functional teapot. The Mohawk hairpiece is the lid. The bust and teapot head are life size. 24" high, 24" wide, 12" deep. *Collection, Racine Art Museum, Racine, Wisconsin. Photo, Phil Schadesma*

Chapter 3
How Ceramic Teapots Happen

Buy one teapot, use it or display it, and enjoy it. But think about how it came to be. Is there a story behind it? Why did the artist choose that design, that shape? The specific materials and glazes? What is there about it that attracts you compared to a teapot that you pass up? What is there about it that makes it valuable to you? And perhaps to other collectors?

It's possible to collect teapots without thinking about how they were made. However, you can appreciate them more if you understand how and why they exist. Knowing processes will help you recognize good craftsmanship that reflects in the quality, the cost, and salability of a piece.

Throughout the book, the process for making a teapot of the specific materials chosen is briefly shown… not so that you will become a ceramist, a glass blower, or a metal or wood worker, but so that you can better appreciate the thought, expertise, and work involved. Before reading further, look at a teapot and ask yourself: Do I understand what went into making this and why it exists? What is there about a teapot that challenges the artist compared to making a bowl, a vase, or a dish, for example?

If the piece is to be functional, hold and pour water, the potter must wrestle with several elements working together to create a harmonious whole. The spout must be positioned so it doesn't overflow when the pot is filled. The handle must be comfortable and at an angle so that it will discharge the water from the spout when held. The lid should not fall off when the pot is tilted. The pot's weight must be balanced when the pot is lifted, and the pot must sit well on the table.

With all that, it should be elegant, unique, and have a pleasing finish. If it is to be functional, the material and glazes must be non-toxic and not leach minerals into the water. If the pot is metal, the handle has to be insulated so the hand is not burned when it is held.

With non-functional, or dysfunctional teapots, those considerations are not so important. They apply to pots that are purely collectibles and fall into the sculpture category. They may be made of wood, fabrics, and myriad imaginative materials shown in Chapters 8, 9, and 10.

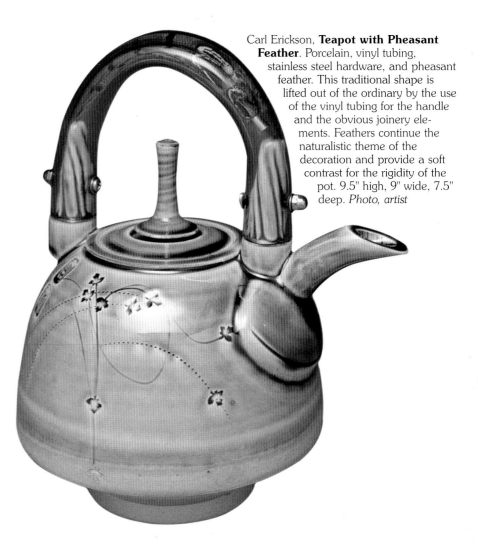

Carl Erickson, **Teapot with Pheasant Feather**. Porcelain, vinyl tubing, stainless steel hardware, and pheasant feather. This traditional shape is lifted out of the ordinary by the use of the vinyl tubing for the handle and the obvious joinery elements. Feathers continue the naturalistic theme of the decoration and provide a soft contrast for the rigidity of the pot. 9.5" high, 9" wide, 7.5" deep. *Photo, artist*

The majority of teapots are made of clay and illustrate a boggling range of artistry, techniques, and imagination. The demonstrations presented are an overview of a process so the reader/collector can better appreciate the steps involved in its creation. They are not offered as detailed how-to procedures. Other teapot makers may glean ideas and inspiration from seeing what their peers have done and how.

Collectors may have a new vocabulary that will improve the dialog and understanding between those who create, and those who sell teapots. In addition to an overview of types of clays, you will see how a pot is made using slabs, the potter's wheel, achieving textures, painted, etched, and glazed surfaces.

The Idea

Ceramists work in different ways but, inevitably, the first thing the potter must do is "see" the pot in his or her mind's eye. Many people will sketch their visions in various stages of completion striving to emulate a two dimensional sketch in three dimensions. Alternatively, they may make rough drawings of parts, make them in clay, and assemble them. The sketches may be painfully detailed or casually rough. They may be made using a CAD (Computer Aided Design) program, showing all sides, dimensions, and elevations.

The Materials

The next decision involves the appropriate clay to be used. Raw clay from the earth must be processed to be used for pottery. Potter's clays consist of earthenware clays, stoneware, and porcelain clays. Their properties vary in firing temperatures possible, colors, and textures.

Earthenware

"Earthenware" clays range in color from white to terra-cotta, with textures that vary from smooth to rough. They can be fired to about 2050° Fahrenheit. Earthenware clay will melt if fired to the higher temperatures used for porcelain. Most potters buy clay manufactured from a range of materials to yield specific characteristics. A few may dig and process their own clays.

Clays that are tan, brown, or brick color contain iron oxide as the coloring agent. Clay colors, without iron oxide (or minimum amounts), are from gray to white. Earthenware clays are porous and somewhat fragile but their color range may be brighter than stoneware. Earthenware clay is popular among potters because its temperature range is constant for all glazes, it is smoother, and uses less fuel than some other clay choices.

Sandy Duval's page from her sketchbook. An artist often captures ideas that may become full teapots or portions of them. Duval frequently uses architectural imagery and details. Her background as a children's book illustrator is carried into her whimsical teapots. *Photo, artist*

Sandy Duval, **Willimantic Victorian Teapot**. Off-white stoneware, fired to cone 07 with her own stoneware glazes over a painted black underglaze outline. Slab and hand-built. Her eye for architectural detail resulted in this teapot when her town conducted a Victorian house tour. 10" high, 8.5" wide. *Photo, artist*

Stoneware and Porcelain Clays

"Stoneware" clays range in color from brown stoneware to white porcelain. Coarse stoneware may contain grog which consists of crushed bricks, fine broken pulverized pottery, or coarse sand. Grog yields textures and reduces shrinkage during the drying and firing processes. Porcelain clay results in a smooth surface when it is fired to the high temperatures of 2200° to 2300° Fahrenheit. Stoneware and porcelain are non-porous, not too fragile, and muted colors are possible.

Because porcelain clays do not have grog, they have a high shrinkage rate, making them difficult for beginning potters to use. Much of the work will crack in drying and there is a high "mortality rate" in the kiln when working with these clays.

Considerations, Techniques, and Procedures

Pottery, or ceramic, teapots can be made using one or several basic construction procedures. These include, slab building, coil build up, molds, pottery wheel, hand building, construction, with many combinations and variations. The shapes that can evolve purposely, or accidentally, are limitless.

The clay shape usually begins by building the main body first, then adding the handle, spout, and legs. After the initial clay shape is formed, the pot has to be dried, fired, and glazed, or painted. Each procedure involves thought, time, experience, artistic talent, expertise and, yes, a lot of chemical and technical knowledge. When considering a ceramic teapot for use, for collecting, and for gift giving, understanding what goes into it makes the purchase more enjoyable.

Following are enough methods to provide a working vocabulary of pottery making generally, and teapots specifically. A bowl, a dish, a platter is relatively simple to make compared to a teapot.

If the pot is to hold water, steep tea, and pour without dripping or losing its cover, the artist must consider the optimum placement of each element: spout, lid, and handle. The weight and heft of the piece, and its aesthetic appeal must all be factored in.

If a spout end is below the surface of the top of the pot, water will spill from it when the pot is filled. The handle must be positioned so it is balanced when the pot is poured. The lid should be set so it will not drop out when the pot is tipped. The handle must be comfortable to hold, not too small so a hand won't fit around it, not so large that it throws the pot off balance.

Carl Erickson believes that a pot should be functional along with concept and artisanship. His teapots are meant to be used, so he has placed the spout high enough to allow the pot to be filled. The steep undercut and narrow foot purposefully lift the pot as if on a pedestal. The knob, thrown in one piece with the lid, seems to float as it hides the vent hole.

Hwang Jeng-daw, **Piled Stones Teapot**. 2003. Slab built parts assembled. Natural ash glaze, cone 10 reduction firing in a wood kiln. Today's sculptural teapots can be any size and form. This outdoor sculpture in Estonia has a human gesture and exudes fun and humor. 39.5" high, 21.6" wide, 13" deep. *Photo, artist*

Drying and Firing

After the clay is shaped, it is allowed to air dry. When it is partially dry, the clay is deemed "leather hard". It is firm enough to hold the form but still soft and smooth enough so that knives can be used to cut smooth designs into the clay. Then it undergoes the first firing, called the "bisque" firing that makes it hard and light colored. The bisque "clay body" can be endlessly decorated by incising designs with a knife or adding clay relief areas. A glaze surface may be added during this firing or subsequent firings. It's not unusual for a pot to undergo several firings.

Most pottery is fired in a kiln, a special oven in which many pieces are stacked at one time. Another way to fire pottery is called Raku, which involves firing a piece at about 1900°, removing it from the kiln while it is still red hot, and allowing it to air cool. A Raku firing may be in anything from an electric kiln to a coal, wood, gas, or oil-fired kiln built in one's back yard.

Raku is generally made from stoneware clay and fired only to the bisque stage so it is always porous and fragile. Potters find it attractive because the Raku firing gives a smoky effect and crazed glazes not possible in regular firing.

Raku ware, now known worldwide as a ceramic technique, was founded by Raku Chojiro in the 16th century in Japan and has carried through fifteen generations of Raku family of potters, over 450 years, as a unique ceramic tradition. There is a Raku Museum in Japan next to the home where the Chojiro family lives.

Colorants and Glazes

The teapot maker must decide how a pot is to be finished early in the creative thinking and decision making processes. The clay chosen will dictate the kind of surface finish one can apply. Techniques and examples for decorating may include one or more of the following: incising, carving, mold casting, texturing, sgraffito, colored pastes, waxes, paints, pencil, and whatever else the creative potter finds that works.

During the firing process, adding different chemicals results in varied final surfaces. These chemicals may be salt glazes, soda ash glazes, and so forth. You will note that many captions state that the pot is fired at cone 06, or cone 07 for example. That means that Pyrometric cones are placed in the kiln with the pots. When the tip of the cone bends, it indicates how much heat has been absorbed. Specific clay bodies, glazes and decoration products, are expected to be fired to a cone number, or within a range of numbers. It's akin to testing the doneness of a roast in an oven with an oven thermometer. In a kiln, the cone does the trick and one watches for its deformity through the kiln's peephole.

Of course, with non-functional teapots, the practical considerations can be ignored.

Martin Meisel, **Baby Grand Teapot**. Raku clay. Slab construction. The artist, who is an architect, was inspired by the wedge-shaped East Wing of the National Gallery in Washington, D.C., by I. M. Pei. 9.25" high, 6" wide, 4.25" deep. *Photo, Pasha*

Richard Notkin, **Cube Skull Teapot: (Variation #27**). 2002. Yixing series. Stoneware. Notkin emulates the colors, textures, and semi-satin finish of Yixing clay bodies. Yixing clay comes in colors, brown, red, and purple with variations. Slab and hand-built. 7.25" high, 6.3" wide, 3.25" deep. *Courtesy, Garth Clark Gallery, New York, New York. Photo, R. Notkin*

Techniques

Knowing the materials used in ceramic teapots is essential to the artist. But materials alone do not a teapot make. The basic building techniques are shown along with finished examples. The shape is a clue to the techniques used. A flat sided teapot will probably be hand built with slabs and molds. A rounded shape would most likely be thrown on a potter's wheel. Both of these methods can be combined with others. The "growth" of a teapot is fascinating to see under the facile hands of an experienced potter.

Slab-Building

If you've never seen a teapot created from scratch, you may be perplexed by how all the parts are designed, assembled, and finished. The slab-building technique is a simple concept. Slab-building, and wheel-thrown teapots (page 46) account for the development of the majority of traditional, and non-functional ceramic teapots. The procedures may be combined with hand building and construction.

Christie Beniston demonstrates the slab building process that results in hand made, hand painted, one-of-a-kind teapots. Once you've seen how the flat slabs of clay are made and assembled, any mystery will be cleared. You will be able to identity teapots made by the slab-building process.

1. Christie Beniston demonstrates her method for making a slab-built teapot. She makes cardboard templates from a pattern of each piece first drawn on paper. She rolls out clay slabs to the desired thickness then cuts the clay pieces to the shapes of the templates.

2. The front and back of the teapot will be softly curved. She uses an extruder to produce a clay "tube" which is flattened and then shaped around a core of rolled paper. One will become the front, the other will be the back panel of the teapot. Each "tube" is sliced vertically and positioned at the front and back of the side slabs.

3. The parts are adhered with "slip" which is a liquid clay, much like using glue on wood. A bottom and top piece are added. An oblong is cut the from the top piece for the lid.

4. The spout is added and worked in with the slip to adhere it She has prepared two handles so she has a choice of which she wants to use. The handle is attached and a decorative element is placed on the lid for lifting it.

5. The clay is soft at this point and must be propped with rags tied onto pieces that might droop. Before drying completely, under paints are applied and sgraffito lines are etched into the leather-hard surface. It is air-dried, then it will be bisque fired to cone 04. After the first firing, additional paints and a clear overglaze are applied, then fired a second time to cone 06.

6. Christie Beniston holds the finished teapot that she has painted with a combination of low-fire paints and glazes. *Photo series, Dona Meilach*

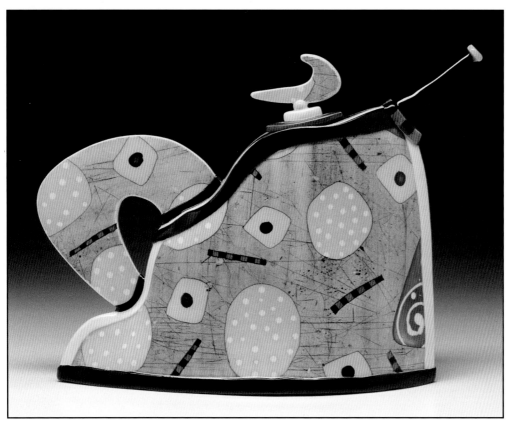

Barbara Chadwick-Bland, **Joy Ride**. Slab and hand-built porcelain. Fired in an electric kiln to cone 09. Whimsical hand painting and overglazes. 8.5" high, 12" wide, 5" deep. *Photo, artist*

Elizabeth F. Keller, **Cattail Cluster Teapot**. Earthenware slab construction. Different textured matte and glossy surfaces help define the cattail strands from the leaves. 8" high, 9" wide, 6" deep. *Photo, Bill Edmonds*

The Coil Method

Vessels and pots made by the coiling method were found in early archeological sites. Beginning students in pottery may start with a pot made by rolling or extruding long snake-like coils of clay and laying them in a circle one atop another until a desired wall of clay results. The potter smoothes the wall by using a moist sponge, hands, and smoothing tools until the shape and surface they want are achieved. Ricky Maldanado's pot is built up in this way. Round, conical, conoidal, box, and abstract shapes can be formed, but it takes time, patience, and experience to make walls of uniform thickness compared to making teapots by slab or wheel-thrown methods.

Another beginner's method is the "pinch pot" where a small slab of clay is shaped into a cup like form and "pinched" at the corners to hold it together. Coil-built and pinch techniques can yield elegant and different vessels but only a few teapot makers use these methods. It is too time and labor intensive.

Ricky Maldonado, **Magdalena**. Coil built. Coils were one of the earliest methods of clay construction. Rather than using slabs of clay, the form is created by rolling moistened clay into snake-like coils and stacking the coils in rows on top of a flat base. As coils are added to the stack, the potter presses them together by hand. He shapes the pot by working the outside with a wooden paddle and other instruments, and holding a block, hands, shaped tools, and damp sponges on the inside to retain the shape. The exterior surface is then rubbed smooth and polished before firing. Maldonado applies each dot by hand using designs from Native American cultures. 15" high, 16" wide, 12" deep. *Collection, Gloria and Sonny Kamm. Photo, Imagination*

Teapots From Molds

Using a mold for making teapots has several advantages over building with slabs and coils. Once a shape is made and a mold taken from it, the mold may be used to reproduce the form infinite times. The clay walls are uniform, which reduces problems in firing that are ever present in slab built pots.

Essentially, commercial teapots are made by using molds. A company may produce only a few teapots from one mold and sell the pots as "editions" just as prints are pulled from a lithograph stone and numbered as editions. By limiting the number of items made from one mold, and destroying the mold, the finished items have greater value to a collector than a process that produces thousands of the same item.

There are two ways to use molds. One is to roll out 2 clay slabs (as shown) and press them into the 2 halves of the mold. The other method is called "slip casting." The mold, which may be made from two pieces to dozens of pieces, depending on the complexity of the original form, is held together by large rubber bands. The clay slip (liquid clay) is poured into the mold and left in until about 1/2" of the slip has hardened against the mold. The remaining liquid slip is poured out, and the 1/2" clay layer hardened against the mold is allowed to dry.

The teapot artist may produce one or several items from a mold, but each pot may be hand finished with additional shaping, glazing, or decorating, so they are one-of-a-kind.

Andi Moran demonstrates how a clay pot is made from a mold. It involves two steps: 1) after the original form is constructed, a two-piece plaster mold is cast. 2) after clay is formed in the two-part mold, the two halves are combined. Additional enhancements can be added to the emerging teapot. It can be carved, etched, burnt, and pieces can be added.

Farraday Newsome uses both the potter's wheel and molds for her teapots. Susan Beiner uses molds to create the repeat hardware elements for detailing her teapots.

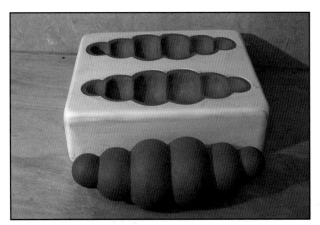

1. Andi Moran makes a two-part plaster mold from an original object. To create additional forms, a clay slab is pressed into the mold and smoothed with a sponge. When the clay is stiff, the two halves are scored, slip is added, and they are joined. These become the teapot body. *Photo series, artist*

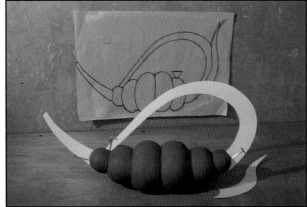

2. To determine the exact size, shape, and placement of the teapot's handle and spout, poster board pieces are cut and placed against the volumetric body. The patterns will be transferred onto a piece of cloth to show where the extruded handle and spout will be laid out.

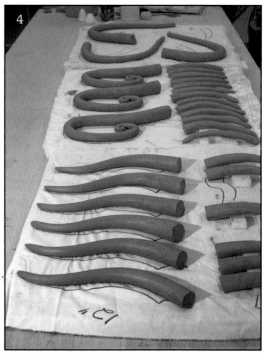

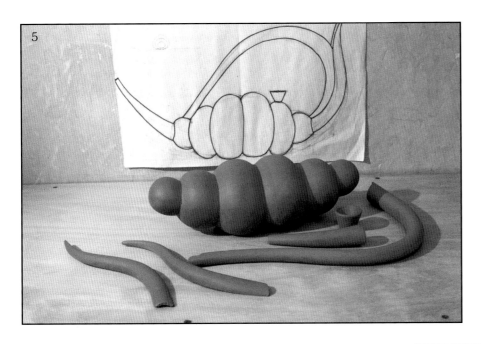

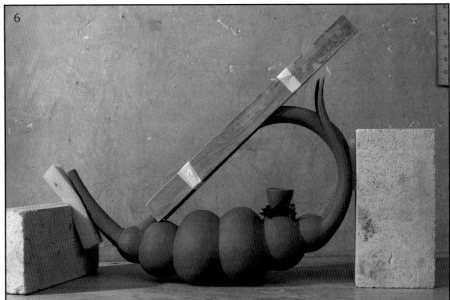

3. Andi Moran pulls lengths of clay from an extruding machine. They will be cut and tapered for the handle and spout.

4. The extruded pieces are laid out on a piece of foam covered by the traced patterns. When the clay stiffens, individual pieces are further shaped by adding and subtracting clay.

5. The completed pieces are added to the teapot body by scoring surfaces to be joined, and adding slip. A small square is cut for the lid opening and edges are beveled to hold the square in place.

6. Props hold the pieces in place and prevent warping through the drying process and under the kiln's heat.

Andi Moran, **Teapot II**. The glazed teapot. White earthenware fired to cone 04 and finished with terra sigillata and glaze. This is from her Subterranean Teapot series inspired by botanical forms she discovers while gardening. 12" high, 17" long, 5" deep. *del Mano Gallery, Los Angeles, California. Photo, artist*

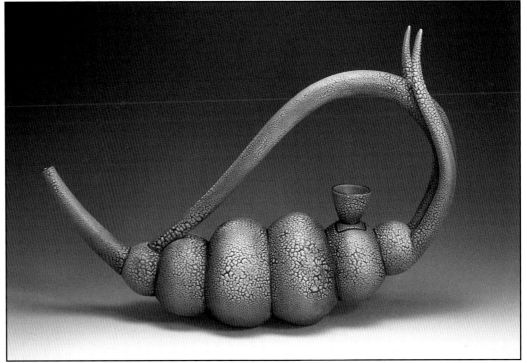

Using A Potter's Wheel

The potter's wheel consists of a flat, horizontal disk that revolves on a vertical spindle. A ball of clay is centered on the disk, and, as the spindle is made to revolve, the pressure of the hands or tools shapes the clay. Mainly, items with round and cylindrical shapes are made on a wheel. The shapes can be wide or narrow, depending on how the hands work the clay as it revolves. The shape can be removed from the wheel and further manipulated and altered, subtracted from, and added to. The process of using a potter's wheel is referred to as "throwing." Potter's wheels date back to Egyptian times, possibly as early as 1500 BC (they are mentioned in Homer's Iliad). Then a young boy powered them, later a foot pedal was used. Today's potter's wheels may be motor driven, or rotated by kicking a foot pedal attached to the spindle.

Ceramists who use potter's wheels make it look easy, but it takes practice, and strength, to become proficient and throw the shapes you want with consistent wall thickness. Various surface designs can be etched into a pot while it is turning, such as parallel lines of different widths. When the turning is complete, the pot can be removed and further carved or embellished, and a spout and handle added.

Farraday Newsome uses wheel throwing for the teapot body, then mold making for additional shapes.

2. The clay spout is also wheel thrown.

1. Farraday Newsome. The teapot body begins to emerge from a clump of clay as the potter spins the potter's wheel and shapes the clay with her hands. *Photo series, Jeff Reich*

3. The spout is attached by scoring the surfaces to be joined, adding slip and smoothing then using the fingers and any necessary tools to make a seamless joint.

46

4. She will add seashells, birds, and other forms made from plaster molds she has created. A slab of clay is pressed into a one-part mold of a seashell.

5. The clay is removed from the mold. It will be trimmed. Other objects will be mold formed also.

6. The seashell is adhered to the body of the teapot on to another curved slab she has added to give additional shape to the pot.

7. A bird, and a half moon, also made from molds, and a handle are added. The piece will be dried, fired, and decorated.

Farraday Newsome, **Clarity of Heart**. 2002. Glazed terra-cotta, wheel-thrown and manipulated, and molded items added. This is the other side of the teapot in the progressive photos. 9" high, 12" wide, 9" deep. *Photo, Jeff Reich*

Farraday Newsome, **Night Clouds Teapot**. 1996. Glazed terra-cotta, wheel-thrown and painted. 16" high, 16" wide, 8" deep. *Photo, Jeff Reich*

Farraday Newsome, **Green Teapot with Fruit and Shells**. 1996. Glazed terra-cotta, painted and colored. 8.5" high, 10" wide, 14" deep. *Photo, Jeff Reich*

Joan Irvin, **Dragon Teapot**. Glazed porcelain with platinum luster. The teapot body is wheel thrown and texture is added. The spout is also thrown and shaped on the wheel, then extra clay is modeled for the head. and attached to the spout. Other elements are hand-built. 4.5" high, 8.75" long, 4.5" deep. *Photo, artist*

Susan Beiner, **Fruitful Teapot**. Porcelain. Hardware items molded and assembled. Molded fruit and other natural objects symbolize growth and change. 10" high, 8" wide, 6" deep. *Photo, Susan Einstein*

Working with Textured Slabs

Surface textures on teapots add interest and character. Many potters use a variety of tools to create indentations, scratches, etching, and other markings on their pots. One efficient method is to add designs to the wet clay while it is spinning on the potter's wheel.

Another method is to use stamps on clay slabs. A stamp is anything that will indent the wet clay. In the following examples, you'll be able to identify some textures, others are randomly applied, and one area may have two or more stamping tools overlaid.

Sandy and Bob Kinzie have developed a unique method for achieving a consistent, but always different, texture for their pots. They begin with a tall piece of clay, then turn it on the potter's wheel until it is a large circular clay cylinder that is the same thickness from top to bottom. The finished cylinder is usually 5-feet long and 8 to 12 inches high when it is cut and released from the wheel. The less experienced potter's cylinder may be thicker on the bottom and slightly uneven all over.

This technique, says Sandy Kinzie, is the only way to make the textures they like to use. Once the clay slab is removed from the wheel and laid out, Sandy may cut pieces, then alter them slightly by stretching the clay. This expands the spaces in the texture creating a different effect.

Four of Sandy's textured pots that follow illustrate the results. Other artists' teapots illustrate innovative applications for stamping and texturing the clay.

In addition to stamping, textures can be made by "combing" the clay for a striated effect, by poking an instrument into the clay, either overall, or in selected areas, by adding small dots of slip with a brush for a raised dot effect, even impressing the imprint from a ridged tire, a gear, a kitchen tool, or the design of a fly swatter into the clay.

1. Bob Kinzie makes evenly textured clay teapot cylinders using the potter's wheel. The textured cylinder is flattened into a slab that is cut into the sizes needed to make teapots, much like using fabrics for sewing. Clay textured with this method is more precise and time saving than texturing by hand. *Photo, Sandy Kinzie*

2. A tall cylinder is thrown on the wheel, then textured by holding a metal comb or patterned wheel against the clay as it turns, resulting in an overall texture. *Photo series, Sandy Kinzie*

3. When the desired size has been reached, it is dried lightly with a blower until the form is rigid enough to handle. Then one side is cut vertically and released from the wheel (it has no bottom).

4. It is then carefully lifted.

5. The resulting slab is laid out flat on a table.

51

Sandy Kinzie, **Ovoid #1**. Made from a textured thrown slab. 8" high, 9" long, 3" deep. *Photo, artist*

6. A variety of textures and effects can be achieved with different tools, the addition of wet clay, and the amount of drying and expansion. It takes a skilled potter to throw a thin and uniform cylinder on a wheel and manipulate a texturing tool as the clay turns.

7. Sandy Kinzie develops a 1/4-circle geometric shaped teapot with pieces of clay cut from the textured slab. The spouts and handles may or may not be textured. *Photo, Bob Kinzie*

Sandy Kinzie, **Pillow Teapot**. Made from a textured thrown slab. 7" high, 6" square. *Photo, artist*

Sandy Kinzie, **Quarter Circle**. 5" high, 9" wide, 2" deep. *Photo, artist*

Sandy Kinzie, **Checkerboard**. A two color "loaf" of checkerboard clay was made, then "sliced" and laminated to white clay for the stepped checkerboard effect. This is a totally hand-built piece. 7" high, 3.5" wide, 1.5" deep. *Photo, artist*

Stamped and Hand Carved Designs

Steve Salisian uses a variety of techniques and ideas to make his incredibly detailed and ornate pots, perfected over more than twenty-five years since he was first smitten by the teapot's potential. He says, "It is a passion, fascinating, and challenging. Forming methods include wheel throwing and hand building. Surface decorations are often derived from natural objects such as shells, pinecones, seedpods, ferns, and fossils. Lace, fabric, metal, wood, and other found objects are used to impress designs and carve into the soft clay."

Salisian combines the teapot body, spout, handle, neck, and lid, into both a decorative and functional object. His pots may be variations on a basic shape but no two are alike. Special emphasis is placed on the teapot's textures and the ornate design of the handle, without compromising the pot's utility and the handle's strength and comfort.

After the finished pieces air dry, they are bisque fired to 1800° Fahrenheit. The porous bisque ware is then glazed and fired again to 2300° Fahrenheit. This high firing matures the glaze, and the clay body becomes hard and vitrified. Percentages of metallic oxides, such as copper, cobalt, and iron, are added to the glaze for variations of blue, green, and other shadings.

Salisian readily acknowledges that he constantly strives to improve his techniques, yet only about 60% of the pieces survive the final firing. Many are lost and discarded because of flaws in the glaze, cracks, warp, and other unpredictable aberrations of the clay and firing processes.

Gina Freuen uses impressed textures in her unique teapots but in a different way than Salisian. She says, "The teapot form has always maintained my focus because of the intricacy of its parts and the gesture that is created as the form develops. Textures are made from whatever works. Slabs and wheel thrown sections are combined, then stained to enhance the overall line and grace of each piece."

Steve Salisian puts the finishing touches on two teapots. Next step is the bisque firing.
Photo series, Nhulan Salisian

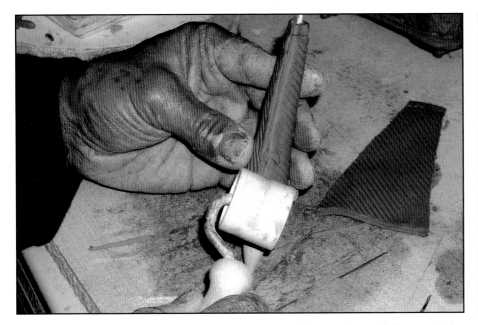

Salisian joins the seam for a clay spout by using slip to hold it together and then attach the spout to the pot. The linear texture was made with a piece of rubber tire.

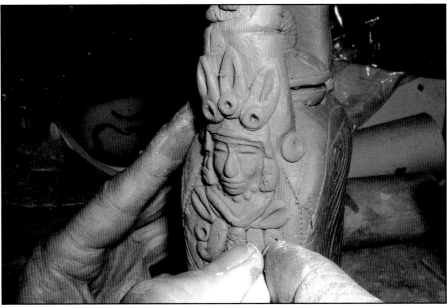

Details added to the front of the body are modeled by hand using fingers and clay modeling tools.

Three porcelain slab teapots with modeled details must dry completely before the first bisque firing.

Steve Salisian is finishing the items for his Dragon teapot series. He uses wheel-thrown elements and modeled portions.

Steve Salisian, **Dragon Teapot**. Porcelain. Combining form, scale, decoration, and function, presents endless challenges to successfully integrate the elements. *Photo series, Nhulan Salisian*

Gina Freuen, **Quadruped Teapot**. Porcelain white stoneware fired at cone 06 in a gas kiln with moderate reduction environment. Textures are pulled from a variety of items. 12" high, 11" wide, 5" deep. *Cheney Coles Museum, Spokane, Washington. Photo, Don Hamilton*

Minako Yamane-Lee, **Mini-Raku Pot**. Clay textured with dots that represent prayer dots in Japanese. Each dot is carefully applied using slip with the tip of an Oriental brush. Japanese temples, shrines, and gardens inspire her shapes. 5" high, 2.75" diam. *Collection, Annette Morimoto. Photo, Alan Decker*

Carol Ann Wedemeyer, **Pink Detail**. White clay with a textured relief design. 7" high, 8" wide, 7" deep. *Photo, Wilfred J. Jones*

Elaine Pinkernell, **Teapot 2**. Textured clay in browns and beiges. 9.5" high, 9" wide, 4.5" deep. *Photo, artist*

Elaine Pinkernell offers another approach to creating surface textures. She says, "I treat the clay as if it were fabric used in a quilt. Each piece begins as soft slabs of clay (sometimes two different colors) which are torn apart and textured. My texture tools may be home made clay stamps, imported Indian wood cuts, and everyday objects such as bits of wood, buttons, screwdrivers, a meat tenderizer, and more.

"The textured pieces are assembled back into a single sheet of clay laid on a tar paper template, like pieces of a puzzle. This sheet is then used to create a body for the teapot utilizing the stiffness of the tar paper for support. Once the piece is firm the clay is removed from the tar paper backing and a spout, handle, and lid are made and added. The result is a boldly refined form made playful by its richly dressed-up surface. The addition of glazes into the textures enlivens the piece with color and contrast. My teapots are fired to 2300° in a reduction atmosphere."

Elaine Pinkernell, **Teapot 1**. Textured clay in black and white. Close-up shows the details in the various stamped textures. 9.5" high, 7" wide, 3" deep. Detail above. *Photo, artist*

Rollie Younger's Industrial Teapots

Rollie Younger's ceramic *Boiler Teapots* look like metal with symbols of welding, rivets, and bridges, topped off with a metal gauge or wire handle. The ceramic stoneware body with a metallic black/bronze glaze usually rests on a forged metal stand. Though the teapots look as hard as steel, there's a softness and pleasure inherent in them.

The teapots and all their parts are composed of wheel-thrown, extruded, and assembled stoneware pieces. They are sprayed with a bronze glaze, fired to cone 05-06 oxidation. Younger's teapots are made primarily for exhibitions and collectors. He cautions that they should not be set on direct heat and that teapots with copper spouts should not be used for acidic teas. Metal artist Mecki Heussen forges the metal stands.

What is there about making these teapots that fascinates Younger? He says, "A teapot allows me to leap from the functional to non-functional. I can explore the inner space and outer surface, extending the physical limits of its use or symbolism. If it has a handle and spout, it is a teapot. That fact that it is a teapot is pleasure enough."

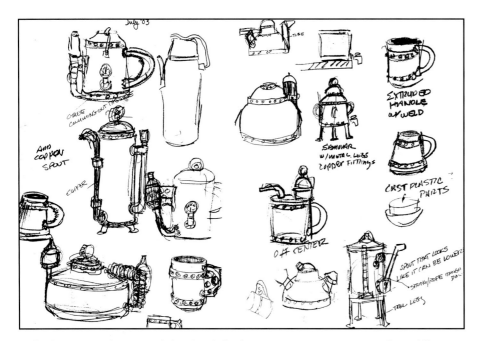

Rollie Younger makes myriad sketches A final piece may incorporate parts from different sketches.

Rollie Younger with several of his ceramic **Boiler Teapots**. They all have metallic glazes and metal gauges. The stands are usually made of forged metal. *Photo, Forrest L. Doud.*

Younger throws the basic teapot parts on a potter's wheel.

When the parts are assembled, the pot is ready for bisque firing.

Younger sprays on the metallic bronze glaze. It will be fired again to set the glaze. *Photo series, Forrest L. Doud.*

Rollie Younger, **Distilled Iced Tea**. Metallic glazed ceramics with metal gauge and forged metal stand. 13.5" high, 11" wide, 8" deep. *Photo, Forrest L. Doud*

Rollie Younger, **High Pressure Teapot.** Metallic glazed ceramics with metal gauge and forged metal stand. 14" high, 14.5" wide, 8" deep. *Collection, Gloria and Sonny Kamm. Photo, Forrest L. Doud*

Frank James Fisher's Tea-Cans

Frank James Fisher calls his teapot sculptures "Tea-Cans." They are somewhere between both objects. They look like a can, but would work well as a teapot. He may design a can by sketching small drawings of the shapes and proportions and then fabricating the parts needed. Alternatively, he may create a group of parts with no final construction plan. He will review the parts and attempt to build a Tea-Can, or two, from them. If he's missing a piece, he may modify what he has or look for pieces in his "parts bone yard." The method often leads to surprising, delightful, and eclectic results.

Why Tea-Cans? He likes the industrial shapes of metal pouring cans. The styles may include gasoline cans, kerosene cans, watering cans, etc. He says "Whether it is a well-manufactured commercial container or a primitive, custom assembled necessity made from bits of leftover metal, each has an honesty in its design. The shape may be dictated by manufacturing processes, materials, costs, or an artisan's ability to shape and solder metal. This is an honest shape created to contain and pour a liquid. Complex curves and sweeping arcs make beautiful design elements, but would be frivolous in this application. The final combination of function versus ease of manufacturing results in a design of great integrity. I don't copy actual cans but rather look to them for inspiration."

Frank James Fisher creates his basic ceramic Tea-Can shapes on the potter's wheel. He uses porcelain clay because it has very fine particles and holds details extremely well. *Photos, courtesy artist*

Industrial metal pouring cans provide the inspiration for Frank Fisher's ceramic Tea-Cans. *Photo, artist*

Fisher uses traditional pottery tools to shape the form. The metal "kidney" tool scrapes a straight line when held at a 90-degree angle to the surface.

Old kitchen tools and odd workshop tools help achieve different surfaces. Misuse of a tool may provide an unexpected advantageous result.

Parts are assembled along with hardware details made from stamps. Fisher covers the clay leaving only a pinhole of air so it dries slowly, perhaps a month or more, before firing. A slow uniform drying process reduces the number of thermal-shock cracks that can occur during the Raku firing process.

Press molds of hinges, bolt heads, bottle caps, etc., are used to create little mechanical add-ons. A plaster mold is made of several items so they can be quickly molded with slip or clay. They give a piece a "manufactured feel" and may include warnings, descriptions, or maker's marks.

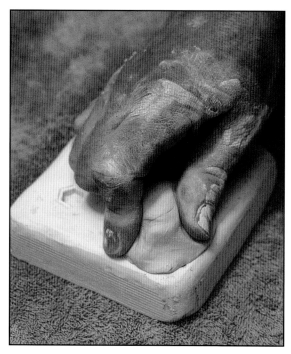

Fisher presses a piece of wet clay into the indented press mold design.

The clay replica of a hinge. The extra clay will be cut away and added to a Tea-Can.

Frank James Fisher, **Mobilgas Tea-Can**. Porcelain. Raku fired. Metal and wood handle added. Glazing is done by a variety of methods. Some areas are masked off with tape to block them from the glazing process. Trained as a painter, Fisher feels that a ceramic object is a perfect canvas. 7.75" high.

Frank James Fisher, **Sinclair Tea-Can**. Porcelain. Each Tea-Can is Raku fired to achieve its final color but Raku carries a degree of unpredictable and unsuccessful firing. Even the glazes are not totally predictable. Raku is the magic ingredient that determines success or failure. 8" high. *Photo, artist*

Ted Neal, **Elevated Teapot**. Soda vapor fired stoneware with steel and nichrome wire. Industrial objects offer a unique inspiration for teapots. 10" high, 5" diam. *Photo, artist*

Ted Neal, **Portable Teapot with Storage Base**. Stoneware and found objects (the luggage clasp at the bottom). Reduction fired Shino glaze, and sand blasted. 15" high, 6" diam. *Photo, arti*

Ted Neal's current work is based on the interpretation of everyday objects that are often discarded or have simply become part of daily life. The industrial forms, textures, and found materials are literal and metaphorical interpretations of things that have traveled from useful object to garbage and, often, back again. Says Neal, "I enjoy looking at our mechanical wasteland for structures that I can reformat around the ceramic vessel."

Nancy C. Frazier, **Pollen Catcher**. 2003. Earthenware hand-built with wire. Primitive shapes and textures provide inspiration for teapots that have a universal history. 8" high, 3.75" wide, 2.25" deep. *Photo, Ted Okello*

J. Dryden Wells, **Industrial Vessel VIII**. 2003. Low fire ceramics. Pieces are made from two part press molds of pipes, rebar, rivets, etc. and thrown, then assembled. When the clay is at the correct dryness, he details the outside with delicately carved images and strategically placed holes to yield the corroded, weathered look he wants. Teapot: 7.75" high, 7.25" wide, 4.5" deep. Cups 3" high, 1.5" diam. *Photo, Josh Smith*

Surface Decoration

The range of glazing materials is infinite. Most artists learn about the intricacies of these chemical mixes on clay by taking basic and/or advanced ceramics classes in college either as young students or as adults beyond normal college years. No matter who, or when, most ceramists continue to experiment with glazes and methods for changing and enhancing clay surfaces to achieve the effects they want. Workshops and classes, held around the year, attract many devotees. There are tried and true glaze recipes but people are always developing new ones, striving for dependable repeat results. Some recipes evolve by accident and yield wonderfully surprising effects that may or may not be duplicated.

Basically, glazes are ground minerals dissolved in water. Pots may be dipped into them, painted or sprayed on, with any or all processes combined. It's the firing that gives glazes their shine and produces the durability required. A pot that is only bisque fired is fragile and porous, and requires a final glazing.

Glazing and firing can have certain risks as to the pot's outcome. The potter learns what clays accept which glazes most effectively and can, in time, reduce the failures that come out of the kiln. However, breakage and problems are a norm that must be factored into the production of a teapot.

In making her tiered teacup teapot sculpture, Dierdre Anderson had to experiment and perform several tests before she created a successful way to stack them. She says, "The elements are wheel-thrown and, when fired with the cups stacked, the rims of each cup would fuse to the foot of the next. Often she had to spend time knocking the units apart from one another with a rubber mallet to remove traces of the glaze. She learned to allow for the increased thickness of the glazed rims and still get a snug fit. She had to smooth the vitreous cup rims and then fire the parts separately. Two feet was the maximum height for stacking on an 8" diameter teapot foot.

Deirdre Anderson, **Tea-Towers**. Bisque dry and ready to glaze. The goal was to organize a practical yet decorative ensemble of stacked tea service parts. The 5-tiered version breaks down into a lidded teapot, two cups, a sugar bowl, and a milk jug. The lid fits either the teapot or the sugar bowl. When stacked, the sugar bowl is at the top with the lid. When unstacked the lid belongs to the teapot. *Photo, artist*

Hank Goodman, **Teapot**. Reduction fired stoneware with ash glazes. This glaze emphasizes the form of each piece rather than hiding or detracting from it. 12" high, 11" wide, 7" deep. *Photo, Tim Burnwell*

Deirdre Anderson, **Lighthouse Tea-Tower**, 5 Tier. Stoneware, fired to cone 10. Dripping glaze provides color. 24" high 8" diam. *Photo, artist*

Hank Goodman uses wood ash collected and recycled into glazes to create the unusual wet look and drip effect on surfaces of his teapots. He collects the ash from people who heat with wood in the North Carolina Mountains, and then sifts it through a screen to remove charcoal and large particulates. He mixes it with nontoxic minerals such as powdered granite, silica, and clay. The powder is suspended into a water slurry and sprayed on the pottery surface. When fired to approximately 2350° Fahrenheit, the glaze melts and makes the clay impervious to liquids.

Sylvia Coppola dips her teapots in glazes for a dual color effect. Ken Ferguson and Ron Nagle use single color glazes over white ware; a clear glaze may be added for a very lustrous surface. Susan Beiner uses a gray glaze to suggest the mechanical look of the hardware elements she has used. Her later pieces (see pages 49 and 74) employ color.

George Roby and Anne Fallis-Elliot opt for black or brown glazes, while Shelley Schreiber uses a traditional Chinese celadon glaze. Jerry Rothman's piece is a white glaze on porcelain. Comparing the effects among these few pots can raise an awareness of the differences and similarities in glazes, how they are accomplished, and what to observe when you look at teapots.

Sylvia Coppola, **Tripod Tea Pot**. White stoneware fired to cone 06 oxidation. Wheel thrown and altered to form tripod feet. Brown, turquoise, and black glaze dipped. 8.5" high, 10" wide, 8" deep. *Photo, Jim Kramer*

Sylvia Coppola, **Twisted Foot Teapot**. White stoneware fired to cone 06 oxidation. Wheel thrown and altered to form tripod feet. Turquoise and black color dipped. 10" high, 12" wide, 8" deep. *Photo, Jim Kramer*

Ron Nagle, **S.O.S**. 2000. Whiteware with red overglaze. 5.5" high, 6.5" wide, 5.5" deep. *Courtesy, Garth Clark Gallery, New York, New York. Photo, Frank Wing*

Kenneth Ferguson, **Tripod Teapot with Hare Heads**. 2003. Black stoneware with green glaze. Hares were a recurring theme in early oriental teapots. 15" high, 10" wide. *Courtesy, Garth Clark Gallery, New York, New York*

George Roby, **Teapot.** 1998, Stoneware with a black matte glaze fired at cone 06. A rectangle at the bottom serves as a contrast to the round teapot shape. It is made by using a length of masking tape to block the rectangular area from the glaze; the tape is removed after firing. 9" high, 6.5" wide, 6" deep. *Photo, artist*

Anne Fallis-Elliott, **Teapot**. 2000. The pots are functional and retain interesting line and form. Black ash metallic glaze. 8.75" high, 6.5" wide, 5" deep. *Photo, Kevin Noble*

Susan Beiner, **Nesting**. 2000. Porcelain, slip cast and hand-built, then assembled. Hardware imagery is a reflection of having lived in Detroit, Michigan. It is constructed like an orange with 4 wedges attached to a central piece which is a giant screw. The inside represents a nest. The outside is the artist symbolically finding her way through the chaos of being in an unfamiliar environment following a move to California. The surface parts consist of conduit that wraps around and within the piece to help contain the space. There are also screws, a bird, and beans among various other parts. *Photo, Susan Einstein*

Shelley Schreiber, **Carved Face Teapot**. Porcelain. Thrown with hand-built spout and handle. Hand carved bas-relief face with mint green glaze. Cone 10 reduction fired. 7.5" high, 9.5" wide, 5" deep. *Photo, artist*

Jerry Rothman, **Ritual Vessel**. Porcelain with white glaze. A monotone teapot shows off the beautiful shape of the teapot. The highly glazed finish picks up reflections and light bouncing from its surface in ever changing effects. 18" high. *Courtesy, artist*

Painting

For many artists, the clay surface offers another canvas on which to display their talents. Often these artists were trained as painters before clay caught their fancy and they have easily bridged the media to bring out the best in their talents.

To Ron Korczynski, painting on clay is as natural and important as eating and breathing. He has a love affair with clay and its potential and never tires of making pots and painting them. After he has created a shape that satisfies him, he makes additional pots from his own molds of Styrofoam and wood. Each one is painted differently using low-fire glazes he finds consistent and dependable. He needn't be concerned with the vagaries of colors, shade, and effects that frustrate, or delight, those who use glazes they mix themselves.

Korczynski's pots subscribe to the Greek theory of *horror vacuii* (horror of a vacuum). No area is left unpainted. His subjects are invariably animal and plant forms infinitely stylized and imagined. Other artists may paint landscapes, seascapes, sporting scenes, flowers, or whatever nurtures their imaginations. A painted piece may also be fired with a clear glaze to give the surface a shine and to preserve it.

Ron Korczynski, **Fish Catcher Teapo**t. 9" high, 7" wide, 3" deep. *Photo, artist.*

Ron Korczynski at work deftly designing every inch of the clay teapots he makes and uses as his "canvas". *Photo, artist*

Ron Korczynski, **Red Bud**. 9" high, 9" wide, 7" deep.
Photo, artist

Ron Korczynski, **Stripe Flower Teapot**. *14" high, 14" wide, 4" deep. Photo, artist*

Ron Korczynski, **Spring Tree**. 8" high, 6" wide, 2" deep.
Photo, artist

Rain Harris, **Three Way Tea**. 2003. Porcelain, slip cast and altered, luster, Plexiglas, 14k gold, freshwater pearls, and beaded fringe. She is fascinated with ridiculous yet elegant objects and the contradictions between the tasteful and the tawdry. 20" high, 11" diam. *Photo, John Carlano*

Bonnie Seeman, **Teapot and Tray**. 2003. Porcelain underglazed and glazed. Her teapots are utilitarian and functional. Shapes and colors are influenced by her environment and interest in botanical forms. 11" high, 6" diam. *Photo, artist*

Rimas VisGirda, **Woman with a Baseball Cap**. Slab built stoneware, engobe, lusters, and china paint. Family, the culture, the machine age, urban environment, the media, and fad and fashion influence the work. 9" high, 12" high, 5" deep. *Photo, artist*

Top Left:
Kurt Weiser, **Opium Teapot**. Top Front. Bottom back. Porcelain.
10.75" high, 13.75" wide. *Courtesy Garth Clark Gallery, New York,
New York*

Left:
Kurt Weiser

Above:
Lidya Buzio, **Untitled Roofscape Teapot XIII-03**. 2003.
Earthenware. 7" high, 10" wide. *Courtesy, Garth Clark Gallery,
New York, New York*

H. James Stewart, **Sorry 'bout the Fence**. Slab built porcelain, carved, stamped, slip textured. The size and power of a horse provide an interesting and challenging form to render. 12.5" high, 11" wide, 3" deep. *Photo, Frank Ford*

Joy Hana Imai, **Gingko Leaf Teapot**. Stoneware, high-fired and soda-glazed with a restrained use of color influenced by Japanese pottery. The leaves are painted and incised black slip surrounded by red shino glaze. 13" high, 9.5" diam. *Photo, Frank Ford*

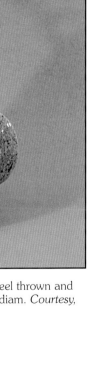

Ralph Bacera, **Untitled Teapot**. 2000. Porcelain. Wheel thrown and hand-built parts assembled and painted. 18" high 12" diam. *Courtesy, Garth Clark Gallery, New York, New York*

Kelly Hong, **Drum-Shaped Teapot with Fish**. Porcelain. Thrown and hand-built. Multiple fired, incised design, and inlaid glaze. Imagery is from nature's forms. She imbues the pots with a sense of animation and sets them upon legs to make them appear as if they could scurry away when no one was looking. Spouts and handles are fashioned after ram's horns, snail shells, or the sinuous curve of a snake's back. 15" high. *Photo, Hap Sakwa*

Gerald and Kelly Hong, **Teapot with Narcissus**. Wheel thrown with hand-built additions, incised design, and inlaid glaze. Collaboration of talents and techniques multiplies the results in beautiful patterns that are serene and rhythmic painted by Gerald, and gracefully shaped Raku pottery by Kelly, all with Asian aesthetics. 15" high. *Photo, Hap Sakwa*

Laney K. Oxman, **Tall Teapot.** 2002. Low fired white ware multi fired using underglaze pencils and stains, enamel decals, and 24k gold luster. 24" high, 20" wide, 9" deep. *Photo, Photo Works*

Zak Zaikine, **Sacred Kiva Tea Se**t. Based on American Indian designs and inspired by the commission to create this set for the chief of the Santo Domingo Native Americans in Santa Fe, New Mexico. *Photo, Owen Kahn*

Creating the *Sacred Kiva Tea Pot* was a life changing experience for Zak Zaikine. The chief of the Santo Domingo Native Americans in Santa Fe, New Mexico, requested twelve ceremonial vessels for one of their rituals. Using the native clay representing earth, Zaikine created vessels that had only a black glaze; no color or marking. The use of monochrome surfaces led to the highly decorated *Sacred Kiva Tea Set* using multi layers of under- and over-glazes. He says, "I felt that the creation bridged two civilizations; joining the old and the new. They awakened primal feelings within me and I felt that I became the Kiva I was trying to make."

Constructivism

Constructivism refers to abstract art that emerged in Europe in the 1920s. First adopted in the Bauhaus period by Mies van der Rohe, it spread throughout Europe and America, and across many media...especially architecture, sculpture, and the decorative arts.

Teapots were caught up in this constructivist web and many forms, alien to traditional teapot makers, emerged. Today, constructing the parts of a teapot can be ascribed to that art movement. From there, it was a short jump to assemblage. The teapots that follow are more construction and assemblage than a pot that appears almost full-blown from clay slabs or by wheel throwing. Yet, the parts may include any or all techniques before they are finally constructed.

Lazslo Fekete, **A New Teapot is Born**. Porcelain. Like a chick breaking out of its egg shell, Fekete brilliantly combines parts of one teapot with a new teapot within. It looks like a puzzle waiting to be solved. 6" high, 8.5" wide. *Courtesy, Garth Clark Gallery, New York, New York*

Kevin Myers, **Totemic Tea**. 1995. Multifired clay with low-fire glaze and china paint; thrown and altered. 76" high, 16" diam. *Collection, Gloria and Sonny Kamm. Photo, Tony Cunha*

Porntip Sangvanich, **Oval Teapot**. 2003. Earthenware. Geometric shapes assembled enable the artist to focus on the simplicity of curved and straight lines, and designs and colors. 8" high, 13" wide, 4" deep. *Courtesy, artist*

Keiko Fukasawa, **Teapot with Cups**. 1995. White earthenware with glaze and luster. 8" high, 13" wide, 6" diam. *Collection, Gloria and Sonny Kamm. Photo, Tony Cunha*

Peter Shire, **Sunburst Accordion**, 1983. Earthenware. An early piece by Peter Shire illustrate shapes he was creating in ceramics. More recent pieces in Chapter 6 are created with found objects and mixed media. 18" high, 18" wide, 6" deep. *Collection, Gloria and Sonny Kamm. Photo, Tony Cunha*

Patrick S. Crabb, **Shard T-Pots**. Cylinders and plates are intentionally broken at the bisque fired stage. Each shard is then painted with unique patterns, and Raku fired in an electric kiln with sage, low-temperature salt, and /or sawdust. In the final stage, the shards are reassembled with epoxy. Approx. 12" high, 16" wide, 6" deep. *Photo, artist*

Vipoo Srivlasa, **Good Friends Triple Teapots**.
Earthenware. Shells made with press molds, applied
to a hand-built earthenware teapot body. Color
glazes. 11" high, 12" wide, 7.5" deep. *Photo, artist*

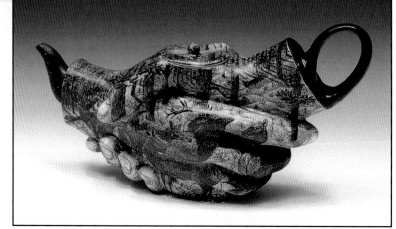

Above:
David Regan, **Agreement Teapot**. 2004. Porcelain. 7.5" high, 12.5" wide. *Collection, Gloria and Sonny Kamm. Courtesy Garth Clark Gallery, New York, New York.*

Right:
David Regan, **Agreement** (other side).

Chapter 4

The Object IS The Teapot

Early potters made teapots that were simple and purely functional. Then some potter with a streak of whimsy, the need to express himself, or to be different, created a teapot that looked like an animal or fish. Not just a painted or etched surface. Rather, the object was the teapot. Perfectly obvious; the body holds the brew, the mouth is the spout, and the tail is the handle. With a little tweaking, and much artistic license, these potters made teapots in the shapes of real and mythical animals, birds, sea forms, and objects they observed in their environments.

Through the years, ceramic artists continued to make unique teapots by fashioning them after familiar items. Commercial ceramic manufacturer's parlayed these ideas into "collectible" teapots and they haven't stopped. British potteries today market teapot houses, toasters, stoves, bathtubs, monkeys, cats… the list is boggling. Teapots made in China in the shapes of pianos, roosters, bears, and owls, are popular collectibles for their novelty value. People who collect these find that the search enhances their enjoyment of places they visit, and the situations that arise. Often, the search is as important and memorable as the object.

Russell Wright, one of America's foremost industrial designers, created several lines of ceramic dinnerware, glassware, and aluminum ware that are now highly sought-after collectibles. His pieces include ceramic versions of vintage luxury automobiles as teapots manufactured by the Steubenville Pottery Co. from 1939 until 1959.

Hall China Company began production in 1903 in Liverpool, Ohio. A single fire process developed by Robert Taggert Hall between 1903 and 1911 was a fortuitous discovery. As a result, Hall China is durable, non-porous and doesn't craze. Collectors seek these old teapots because they are still in relatively pristine condition.

Py Miyao, a Japanese pottery company makes whimsical teapots as kitchen items in the shapes of stoves, sinks, refrigerators, and farm animals.

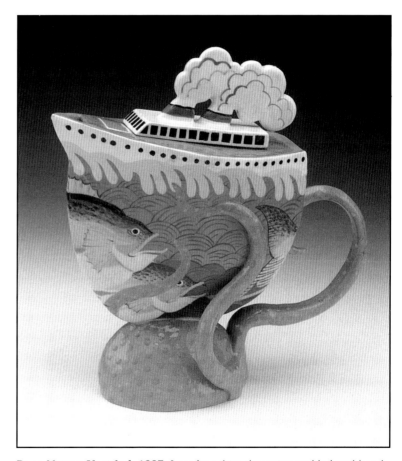

Dana Heister, **Untitled**. 1987. Low-fire white clay using molded and hand-built elements and hand painted with up to five firings. Her inspiration is folk art and miniatures. 7.25" high, 8" wide, 2.35" deep. *Collection, Gloria and Sonny Kamm. Photo, Tony Cunha*

Object pottery pieces from these companies enjoy such popularity as collectibles that books have been written discussing their identifying marks, prices, historical information, and resources. Inveterate collectors of these older pots haunt antique shops, resale shops, garage sales, flea markets, and on-line auction sites for their finds. None of these were one-of-kind. A design likely to enjoy a large market would be molded and multiple copies made from it.

The teapots in this chapter are one-of-a kind. The artists have early pots as their muse and inspiration but each is unique. Many carry an insight into an artist's creative thinking and their special interests. You'll find people, animals, fairy tale characters, political statements, and an amazing array of unlikely objects waiting to grace your table.

David Regan's *Agreement Teapot* (page 88) in black and white shows the artist's expertise in both shaping and painting a teapot. The restrained palette with many tonal shades is a sharp contrast to ceramics pieces that rely on color for their effects.

Dana Heister creates vessels filled with objects illustrating his interest in nature's forms, especially those from the sea. Octopus tentacles surround the teapot in clay for the handle and partial support. The tentacle form is extended around the piece in paint. A yacht is perched quietly above this life filled world below. The spout is at the top front of the boat. Heister's colors and juxtaposition of form and image require careful study to appreciate all that is in the piece

Appreciation of the shapes and painting is required for Jim Budde's and Sergai Isupov's teapots. Both artists deal with anthropomorphic figures in wild, fantastic, imaginative ways, and are completely different from one another….and from anyone else's. I suggested to Jim Budde that his college ceramic students must love him because of his no-holds-barred approach to creating whatever they can imagine.

Red Weldon Sandlin's *The Chinese Quin Teapots* was inspired by a story that was read to her as a child. It was bolstered by watching a Chinese movie as an adult. Her exquisitely hand drawn imagery tells a story metaphorically. Additionally, a book and a teapot appear in almost all her work because they represent containment and are symbols of information. Such symbolism appears again in her *Curiosity of a Monkey*. The teapot rests on a book.

Jim Budde, **Lovely Hula Hands**. 2002. Ceramics, low-fired glazes. Inspired by pre-Columbian ritual vessels and sculptures. 27" high, 17" wide, 7" deep. *Collection, Diane and Sandy Besser. Photo, artist*

Sergei Isupov, **The Time is Coming**. 1997. High-fire porcelain with glazes. Detailed painting with thinned glazes behaves like watercolors. He is well known for his figurative sculpture. Here he has tackled the teapot form as sculpture that provides a surface for his unique artwork. *Collection, Gloria and Sonny Kamm. Photo, Tony Cunha*

Michael Lucero, **Anthropomorphic Teapot, New World Series**. 1994. Earthenware with glazes. 17" high, 16.5" wide, 8.25" deep. *Courtesy, Gloria and Sonny Kamm. Photo, Tony Cunha*

Red Weldon Sandlin, detail of the removable head and a fish motif. The top teapot represents the brother who sucked up water with a straw. *Photo, Charles Akers*

Red Weldon Sandlin, **The Chinese Quin Teapots**. 2003. Hand-built using the coil method, and hand painted. Based on a story about five Chinese brothers. The head is removable. Fired in Chinese blue glazes. 20" high, 5.7" wide, 5.5" deep, plus the book on which the tower stands. *Collection, Gloria and Sonny Kamm. Photo, Charlie Akers*

Carrie Anne Parks, **Founding Fathers**. 2001. Earthenware hand-built, and underglaze painted.
From a series of teapots depicting historical figures. 10.75" high, 11.25" wide. *Photo, artist*

Laura Wilensky, **Autumn Chores**. 2001. Porcelain. Hand-built, hand painted with underglaze and clear glaze fired to cone 10, with additional overglaze fired to cone 18. A story telling teapot representing the artist and her husband doing outdoor chores. He is pulling equipment from the shed. The teapot spout is behind him. The bear that raided a squirrel-proof birdfeeder is represented. 9" high, 10" wide, 9.25" deep. *Storm Photo*

Side view. The artist is shown stacking firewood. The tree at the back is the teapot's handle.

Carrianne Hendrickson, **The Letter**. Sculptural teapot with clay glaze and underglaze. The teapot on the stack of books comes out and is the lid. The spout is behind the pillow on which the woman figure is reclining. (See inset.) It has no handle; it is meant to be held up and poured. The pot does hold water but it is not necessarily a functional teapot. The artist's goal in making teapots is to make it not look like a teapot. She disguises things to trick the eye. 13" high, 16" wide, 7" deep. *Courtesy, del Mano Gallery, Los Angeles, California. Photo, David Peters©2004*

Back view showing the teapot's spout placement. *Photo, artist*

Jack Earl, **Earl's Bean Teapot**. 1994.
Ceramics, painted and glazed. Anthropomorphic symbolism often is based on
historical events and figures that may be
satirical and humorous. 15.25" high,
8.5" wide, 4.5" deep. *Collection Gloria
and Sonny Kamm. Photo, Tony Cunha*

Carol Richter Sils, **Shi Hu's in the Loop**. Porcelain
fired at cone 10 with varied glazes. A "women" teapot
series evolved from a vase and was inspired by her
belief that women carry cultural messages from one
generation to the next. Faces are individually sculpted,
brushed with metallic powders, and lacquered. The
sleeves are the handle and spout. 17.5" high, 6" wide,
4" base diam. *Photo, Bernard Wolf*

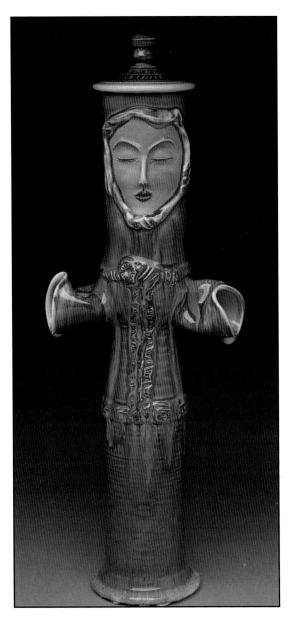

Jim Neal, **Joy 2**. Stoneware.
Given the versatility of clay to
express emotions, Neal's dancer
looks as though she is ready to
move with, or without, music. One
leg is the handle, the other is the
spout. A hand lifts out for a lid. 12"
high, 12" wide, 6" deep. *Photo,
Michael Noa*

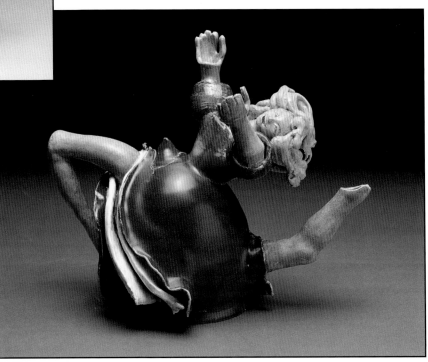

Jane Kelly Morais, **Frida as Teapot**. Earthenware, slips, stains, and glazes. Sculpture as teapots investigates the sameness and meaning of the female form. Each pot in her series is influenced by classical and tribal sculpture of women as powerful figures. 14" high. *Photo, Harvey Kirstel*

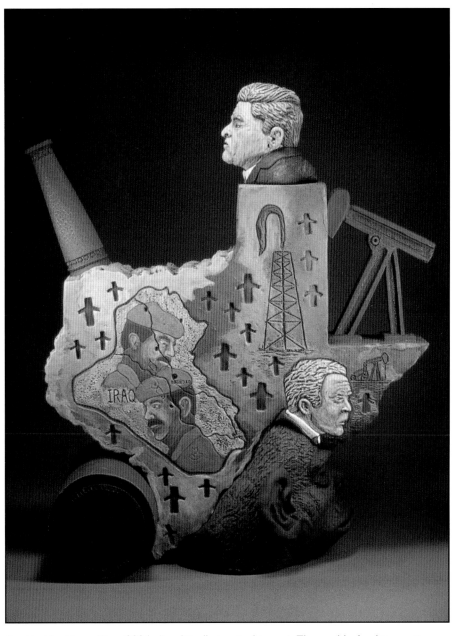

Jim Budde, **Texas Tea**. 2004. A politically inspired teapot. The world of politics as it affects the human condition is hard to escape, so he embraces it through his artistic endeavors. 20" high, 17" wide, 7" deep. *Collection, Gloria and Sonny Kamm. Photo, artist*

Phillip Maberry, **Opium Teapot**. 2002. Whiteware. Mayberry has enjoyed a versatile career perfecting a variety of techniques and materials for decorative ceramics. 15.5" high, 8.5" wide. *Courtesy, Clark Garth Gallery, New York, New York*

Tom Rippon, **Servizio Italiano**. Porcelain, luster, pencil, and acrylic. He likes to take recognizable things and alter their context to upset expectations and keep his viewers alert. Complacency is an enemy. 15" high, 8" wide, 6" deep. *Courtesy, Mobilia Gallery, Cambridge, Massachusetts.*

Lucian Octavius Pompili, **Aegypt.** 1998 5.5" high, 9" wide, 7.25" deep.
Collection Gloria and Sonny Kamm. Photo, Tony Cunha

Rosalind and Barry Hage, **Walking the Walk Through Life**. Low-fire clay and glazes. A combination of wheel-thrown, hand-built, and slab construction. In today's world, the piece represents a statement against obesity. 8" high, 6" wide, 4" deep. *Photo, Barry G. Hage*

Nancy Carmen, **Bend/Ripple**. White earthenware with underglazes and clear glaze. 11.5" high, 10" wide, 9" deep.
Collection Gloria and Sonny Kamm. Photo, Tony Cunha

Animals and Nature as Subjects

Sea creatures, circus animals, insects, flowers, fruit, are all inspiring forms for teapot shapes. Being tuned to "thinking teapots" becomes such an all consuming thought process that artists will look at an object and mentally try to envision it as a teapot. They may conjure a reason for that pot becoming a sculpture. The result may underscore their feelings about a subject or extend their thought to their philosophy, their political leaning, and, perhaps some tragic, or happy event in their lives.

Scott Schoenherr, **Royal Rhino with a Horseshoe Handle**. 1992. Whiteware. Real and imaginary symbols adorn the blanket and the base. 13" high, 10.5" wide, 4.5" deep. *Courtesy, Gloria and Sonny Kamm. Photo, Tony Cunha*

John W. Hopkins, **Ceramic Teapot**. Low-fire clay with luster surfaces. 6" high, 7" wide, 3" deep. *Photo, artist*

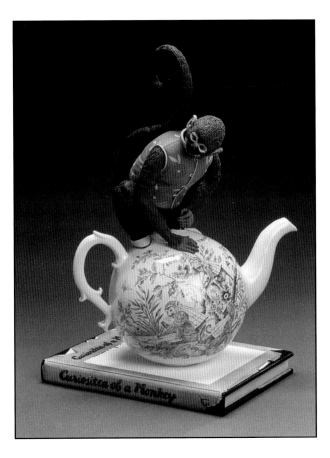

Red Weldon Sandlin, **Curiosities of a Monkey**. 2001. Ceramic. The piece reflects her concern with containment and information. Teapot: 11" high, 16.5" wide, 8" deep. The book is 1.5" high, 10.5" wide, 8.5" deep. *Collection Gloria and Sonny Kamm. Photo, Tony Cunha*

Adrian Saxe, **Irrational Exuberance**. 2001. Porcelain. 8" high, 9" wide, 5.25" deep. *Collection Gloria and Sonny Kamm. Photo, Tony Cunha*

Kathryn McBride, **Dream Journey on the Spike Trail.** 1997. This piece is part of a series of circus wagon tea sets (Circus C'est la Vie) featuring Mother as a circus performer. *Collection Gloria and Sonny Kamm. Photo, Tony Cunha*

Marnia Johnston, **Dragonfly Teaset**. Porcelain with underglazes and stains fired to cone 05 and finished with clear glaze. The insects are assembled after firing. The teapot is 10" high, 11" wide, 6" deep. *Photo, artist*

Oleg and Elena Gorbachevski, **Rhino Teapot**. Clay with glaze and acrylic paints. 7" high, 14.25" wide, 4" deep. *Courtesy, del Mano Gallery, Los Angeles, California. Photo, David Peters©2004*

Unlikely Subjects For Teapots

Ceramic teapots can reflect events, such as Richard Shaw's *Teapot Wedding Cake,* that shows the rejected suitor toppled from the cake. That's a direct scenario that we "read" in good humor.

Teapots can reflect happiness, family values, historical events, modern life…the list is endless. They can simply be enjoyed for their own sake. Shaw's *Dominos Teapot,* with each piece carefully rendered in ceramics, emulates the collages and assemblages of Joseph Cornell's found art assembled pieces of the 50s. There are teapots that represent geometric shapes and may or may not have meaning beyond their challenge of creating them and their esthetic appeal.

Then there are pieces that just happen under an artist's hands. Ron Nagle says, "Humor, eroticism, car, food culture, and ceramic tradition are all part of his mix, but none of it is conscious. I know what I'm doing after the fact, but I prefer not to know what I'm doing before I do it. The choice of a piece's basic color is completely arbitrary, intuitive, or whatever. I like the basic color, and everything else follows."

Richard Shaw, **Rejected By Friend**. The commonplace is combined with the whimsical, and the humorous with the mundane. With the sensibility of a comedian he depicts the old boyfriend toppled while the bride and groom continue with their wedding nuptials. 5.75" high, 7.75" diam. *Courtesy, Mobilia Gallery, Cambridge, Massachusetts*

Richard Shaw, **Domino Teapot**. Porcelain. Cast objects and overglaze with transfer decals create a trompe l'oeil composition. 8.25" high, 5.75" wide, 2.5" deep. *Courtesy, Mobilia Gallery, Cambridge, Massachusetts.*

Claudia Tarantino, **Ready to Slice**. 2003. Porcelain with translucent underglazes with some solid or darker trim color brushed on. The vessel is a springboard for personal expression using organic forms that are universally understood. 6" high, 9" wide, 7" deep. *Courtesy, Mobilia Gallery, Cambridge, Massachusetts.*

Sharon Norquest, **Castle Teapot**. From a teapot series containing architectural elements. The handle is a flying buttress, regular buttresses support the sides, and a stained glass window is highlighted in the center. 9" high, 6.5" wide, 4" deep. *Photo, artist*

Richard Notkin, **Cooling Towers Teapot (Variation #36)**. 2001. Stoneware. Yixing series. 6.8" high, 9" wide, 3.75" deep. *Garth Clark Gallery, New York, New York. Photo, R. Notkin*

Jerry Berta, **Tea Time**. From his Diner Series.
Neon is added. 20" high, 24" wide, 16" deep.
Photo, Phil Schadesma

Anne Kraus, **The Investigative Team Teapot**.
2001. Whiteware. 9.5" high, 11" wide. *Courtesy,
Garth Clark Gallery, New York, New York*

Joan Irvin, **Pipe Dream**. Porcelain with metallic glaze. 7" high, 12" long, 3" wide. *Photo, artist*

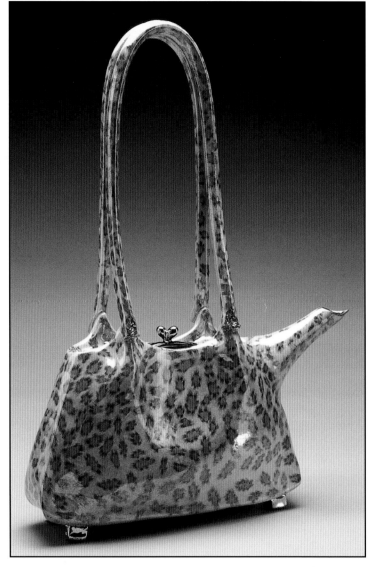

Meryl H. Ruth, **Leopard Tea Purse II**. Terracotta with Majolica. 15" high, 15" wide, 4" deep. *Photo, Robert Diamante*

Erik Gronborg, **Teapot**. White stoneware hand-built from slabs with some use of plasters molds. Inside stoneware glaze, outside low-fire glazes 8" high, 12" square. *Photo, artist*

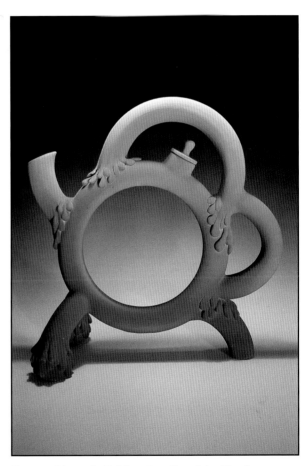

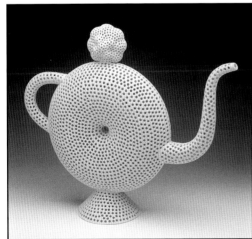

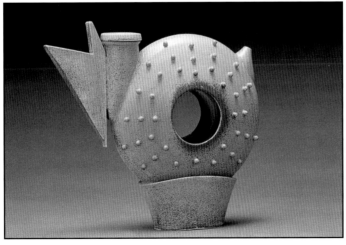

Tony Marsh, **Perforated Teapot**. 1999. White earthenware teapot pierced. Marsh's vessel-based forms incorporate a rich variety of tones and surface treatments. 14" high, 16" wide, 6" deep. *Collection Gloria and Sonny Kamm. Photo, Tony Cunha*

Carol McFarlan, **Teapot**. Porcelain, wheel-thrown and hand-built. Form, simplicity, function, and beauty are combined. The ability to look through the center circle onto another plane is like focusing on a microcosm to see something larger. The pot's surface is perforated with small holes. 9.5" high, 9.5" wide, 2.75" deep. *Photo, Charles Frizzell*

Suzanne Maxwell, **Cold as Ice**. Porcelain. She throws a variety of different shapes including cylinders, cones, bowls, and doughnuts. She will manipulate, alter, and combine components while the clay is wet and workable. Inspiration derives from the parts themselves and how she feels they will work together. 17" high, 16" wide. *Photo, artist*

109

D. Craig Bremer, **The Mad Tea Party**. Sterling silver. Casting, die forming, spinning, etching, and forging. The tea service is based on ideas from a situation in the children's book, *Alice in Wonderland*. They are whimsical and humorous. **Queen of Hearts Teapot**: 13" high, 10" wide, 8" deep. **Mad Hatter Sugar Bowl**: 5.5" high, 4.5" wide, 6" deep. **Hare Creamer**: 9" high, 3.5" wide, 5" deep. *Photo, Bart Kasten of Bart's Art*

Chapter 5
Silver Teapots

Today's silversmiths are using the time-tested techniques and tools employed by our European and American Colonial ancestors. Sure, they have added a few new tools for folding and heating. Still, the silversmiths use only a variety of hammers and stakes, or anvils, to shape or "raise" the metal that enables them to perform their magic.

Silver in its natural state is a very soft metal that requires the addition of copper or other metals to make it harder and stronger. Alloys are formulated to be malleable and ductile so that the artist can shape a sheet of silver or another alloy into the intricate forms associated with jewelry, or raise it into hollowware shapes for teapots and vessels.

Kristin Mitsu Shiga's journey through the creative process for her raised teapot titled *Turf* is an insight into the why's and how's of making a silver teapot. The finished product appears simple and elegant but reaching that result was a complex matter. Shiga, who normally creates elegant jewelry, tested her mettle dealing with the silver metal. Her objectives were to see how many solder joints she could achieve on one piece. How many times could she hit the silver disc with a hammer without it cracking? How could she manage to fit all the pieces of this 3-dimensional puzzle together? How could she make a functional piece of hollowware that transcends the somewhat mundane act of making tea?

Beginning with a ten-inch disc of 18-gauge silver sheet and using traditional raising techniques with only a raising hammer and stakes, she began to work on the teapot that would take nine months to complete. She annealed the metal after each run of hammer blows to relieve the work hardness building within. Each element was carefully hand-fabricated with almost one hundred solder joints including the many pairs of ornamental rivets. "Turf" is a functional teapot that has been exhibited widely and earned honors in several competitions

Michael Banner's teapots are a departure from traditional teapot concepts. They are plain and simple with added graceful, linear, almost gravity-defying sculptural handles.

Kevin O'Dwyer solders silver with a torch in each hand. *Photo, James Fraher*

Kristin Mitsu Shiga, **Turf**. Sterling silver, maple handle and feet, and dyed green hair. This functional teapot has a secret message nestled discreetly inside that says, "Drink More Tea". 10" high, 12" wide, 6" deep. *Collection, Gloria and Sonny Kamm. Photo, Courtney Frisse*

Carrying those concepts still further, Kevin O'Dwyer creates curves and curls like unruly tendrils of hair. Some of his teapots combine silver and gold. O'Dwyer says his "romance with teapots" has been going on for over 20 years. Teapots are playtime for him. Time to experiment with highly reflective textures and patterns, time to create a sense of movement using its flowing art potential, time to explore the dialogue between form and surface.

Cynthia Eid used a new tool to create folds in metal for her fluid silver form, *Convergence*. Generally, her ideas for forms have their roots in her garden, and in the images she discovers meandering through woods and along water's edges. These "souvenirs of nature" are a constant source of inspiration.

Harriete Estel Berman emulates a signed Paul Revere teapot using tin lids from contemporary products. Does this make her teapot more or less precious if one considers that it's the work that matters?

Other metals can be made to appear as silver by plating them; therefore some hollowware is silver-plated and is less expensive than silver. Teapots must be stamped as to whether they are silver or silver plate; the stamp usually appears on the bottom of the pot.

In addition to raising a silver sheet of metal to a desired shape, silver can also be cast; Penny Michelle's teapot jewelry is an example. It is first created in wax. From that wax model a mold is made similar to the process of making molds for creating ceramic replicas. The difference is that silver casting is called "lost wax casting" because the original wax model melts and is burned out during the mold making process. The resulting mold can then be used to make multiples of the original. Michelle's final sterling silver pendants are made by this lost wax casting method.

Paulette Myers, **Ceremony Spirit Rising**. Sterling silver, pearls, 14k gold, and hematites. The bases are aluminum and iron. The design refers to the traditional Japanese Tea Ceremony. Teapot: 7" high, 5" wide, 4" deep. Each cup is 1.5" high, 2.75" diam. *Photo, artist*

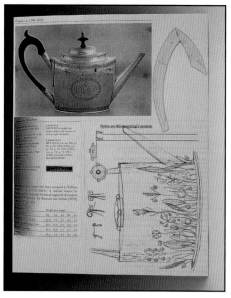

Lydia V. Gerbig-Fast's historical inspiration, preliminary sketch, and a handle pattern. *Photo, artist*

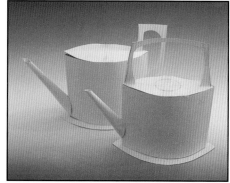

Paper models used for planning the teapot. *Photo, artist*

Lydia V. Gerbig-Fast, **I Went to a Garden Party**. Sterling silver, sycamore, enamel on copper, fine silver, and pearls. 5.5" high, 8.25" wide, 3.25" deep. *Mobilia Gallery, Cambridge, Massachusetts. Photo, artist*

A hand carved maple form was first carved as the basis for shaping the silver teapot body. *Photo, artist*

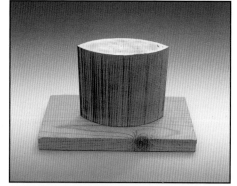

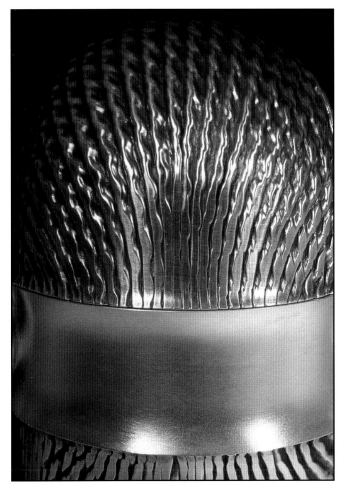

Cynthia Eid, **Convergences** (detail). *Photo, artist*

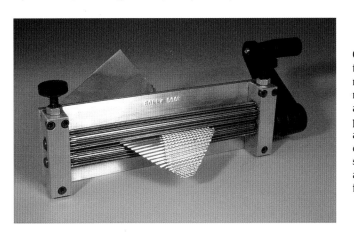

Cynthia Eid uses a tool that textures the metal and produces microfold corrugated and cross-corrugated patterns. There are also special pliers that can accomplish similar effects but not as quickly or uniformly. *Photo, artist*

Cynthia Eid, **Convergences**. Sterling silver, patina, and epoxy. 4.5" high, 3" diam. The fascination with silversmithing is the ability to make a flat, hard form seem fluid through force, determination, and tenacity so that it becomes an object of unity, fluidity, and utility. *Collection, Gloria and Sonny Kamm. Photo, artist*

Dallae Kang, **An Unforgettable Moment**. 1999. Sterling silver and fine silver. The teapot is a bouquet of roses and baby's breath. There are three roses; the middle element in the rose on the right lifts out and functions as a funnel to receive water. The rose on the far left is the spout. The bow is the handle. 6.5" high, 6.5" wide, 5" deep. *Photo, Zack Peabody*

Annie Publow, **Wedding Cake Teapot**. 1997. Sterling silver and Niobium. In addition to the wedding cake inspiration, the piece contains several forms such as the pair of butterflies perched in place of the groom. The butterflies with caterpillar-eaten leaves symbolize the casualties of love that may precede the mature choice of marriage. 7.75" high, 6" wide, 4.5" deep. *Photo, artist*

Helen Blythe-Hart, **Self Portrait as a Funnel-Top Teapot**. Sterling silver, cast glass, and rubber. Each element in this teapot has personal meaning and symbolism. 9" high, 8" wide, 2.5" deep. *Collection, Deutsches Goldschmeide, Haus Hanau, Germany. Photo, artist*

Hyunah Lee, **Greeting.** Sterling silver and smoky quartz. 5.5" high, 3.5" wide, 1.75" deep. *Photo, artist*

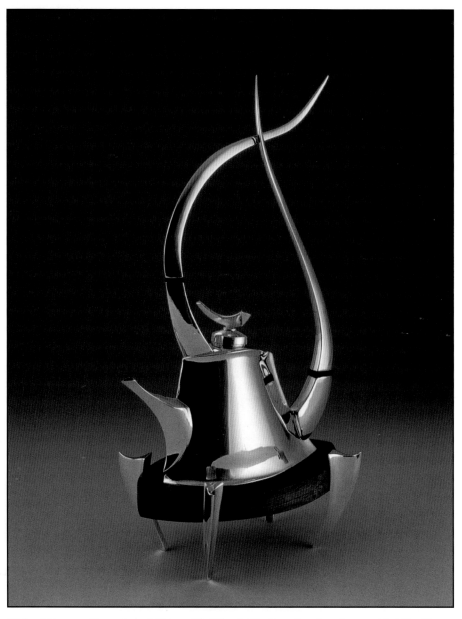

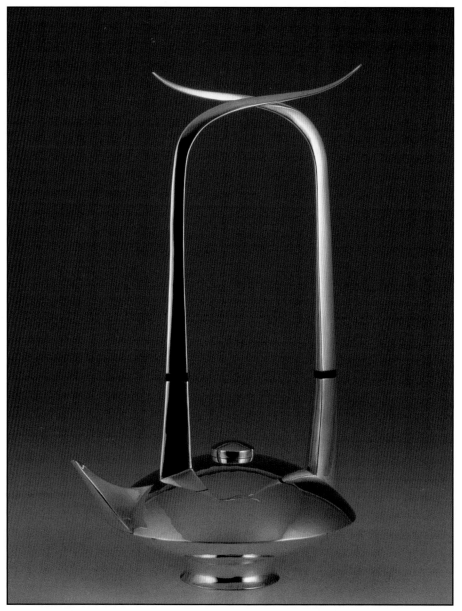

Michael Banner, **Teapot and Tray with Wood**. Sterling silver hand wrought. 14" wide, 11" diam. *Photo, Paul Rocheleau*

Michael Banner, **Pagoda Series**. Hand wrought and raised sterling silver. 17" high. *Photo, Paul Rocheleau*

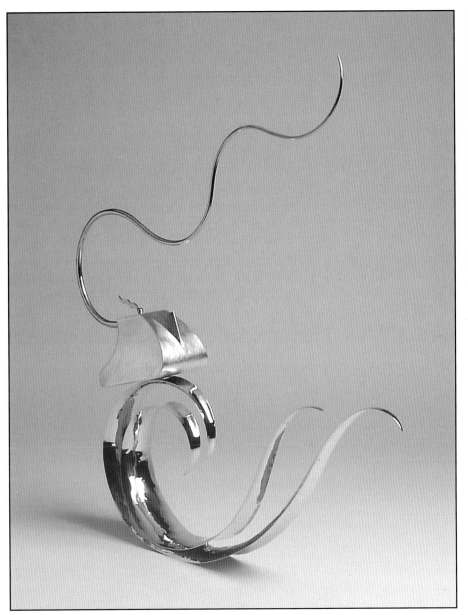

Kevin O'Dwyer, **Teapot on the Crest of a Wave**. Hand fabricated sterling silver with a hand forged gold-plated sterling silver handle. Playful, optimistic, and flowing forms that react and interact with each other. Balance, spontaneity, and the reflective qualities of the materials all play a part in their creation. *Collection, Racine Museum of Art, Racine, Wisconsin. Photo, James Fraher*

Kevin O'Dwyer, **Mad Hatter's Teapot.** Sterling silver hand fabricated and patterned using traditional silversmithing techniques. The arms/handles are hand forged to a high polish in contrast to the patterned teapot base. The piece represents the artist's departure from traditional restraints of functionality. It was inspired by the fanciful vision of the mad hatter's tea party from Lewis Carroll's book *Alice in Wonderland*. 12" high, 8" long, 5" wide. *Photo, James Fraher*

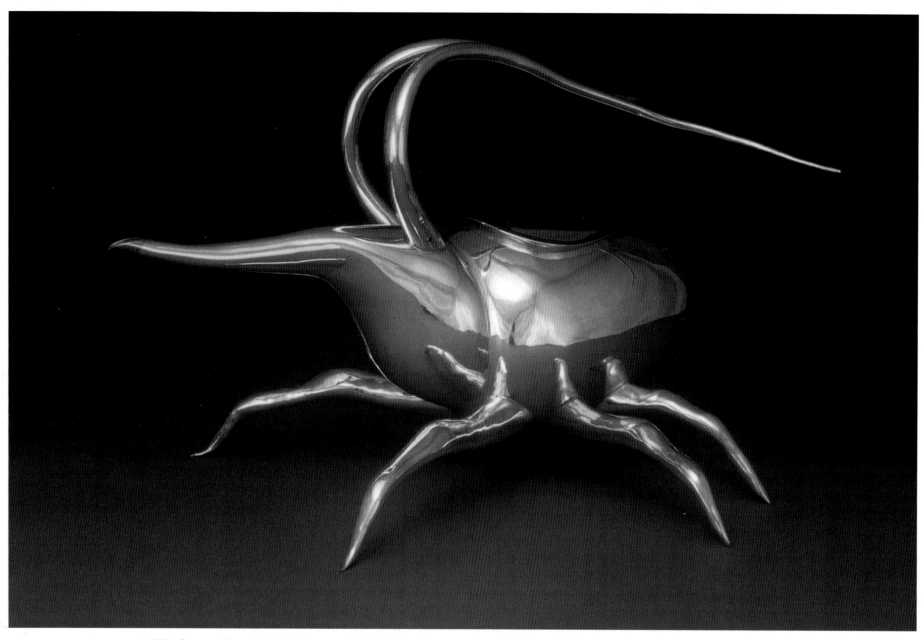

Mike Sharpe, **Teapot**. 2004. Copper and silver plate. The concept was to design a bridge form that might have been inspired by an insect. Insects are feared by some, revered by others, but rarely do people want them on their dinner or coffee tables. Playing with that sensibility resulted in this "bridge" version of a teapot. 11" high, 14" long, 7.5" deep. *Photo, artist*

Boris Bally, **Decision T-Pot**. 1992. Silver with a gold plated interior. The teapot looks like a space ship with two pouring spouts and similarly shaped handles that challenge one to decide which part to hold and which way to pour. 6.75" high, 16" diam. *Photo, Dean Powell*

Wayne S. Sutton, **Zizzer Zazzer Zzuz**.
Sterling silver and anodized aluminum. 12"
high, 9" wide, 3.5" deep. *Photo, artist*

Cynthia Eid, **Rockport II.** Sterling silver and resin
with patina. Inspired by rock formations. 4" high, 6"
wide 1.5" deep. *Collection, Sonny and Gloria Kamm.
Mobilia Gallery, Cambridge, Massachusetts. Photo,
artist*

Helen Blythe-Hart, **Stegosaurus Tea Service** (teapot only). 2003. Sterling silver. Forming, forging, anti-clastic raising, and fold forming. Unlike objects are paired to represent the commonality of the mundane and the absurd: a silver tea server and an ancient dinosaur. 8.5" high, 10" wide, 5" deep. *Photo, artist*

Michele Ritter, **Passion**. 2003. Sterling silver. The center of the passionflower, simulated in silver, becomes the lid for the teapot. Areas of hammered texture contrast with smooth silver areas. 9" high, 7" wide, 6" deep. *Photo, Helen Shirk*

Sarah Perkins, **Cherubfish Teapot**. 2003. Silver, enamel, and amethyst. This tiny gem of a teapot is the result of the artist "playing" with her materials, experimenting, and manipulating them until they are mutually complementary. 4" high 5" wide, 3" deep. *Courtesy, Mobilia Gallery, Cambridge, Massachusetts. Photo, Tom Davis*

Harriete Estel Berman, **"Silver" Preferred**. 2000. Made from multiple panels of tin-plated steel from the bottoms of recycled tin cans. Embossed monogram on the side is from a popcorn tin bottom and another is used for the slightly domed lid. The artist hand carved a 200-year-old piece of maple wood for the handle. 8.5" high, 18.5" wide. *Private collection. Photo, Philip Cohen*

Kye-Yeon Son, **Service for Memory**. Sterling silver and a marble lid. A ritual vessel used for wine in Korea and for tea in western cultures. 6" high, 4.75" wide, 4.25" deep. *Photo, artist & Hyun Soek Sim*

Albion Smith, **Teapot #18**. Sterling silver with 18k gold, chrysoprase, ebony handle with abalone inlay. Pierced overlay with engraving. 5" high, 7" diam. *Photo, Carol Holaday*

Ross Morrow, **Radioactive**. 2002. 6.5"
high, 7.5" long. *Photo, Niki Kavakonis*

Ross Morrow, **Abbots Harbor Light**. 2003.
One from a series of lighthouses that he
interprets as teapots. 9.8" high, 11" wide. *Photo,
Nike Avalon.*

Jeffrey Clancy, **Tea for One**. 2002. Silver and mahogany. The pun is both the object and the title. 6" high, 10" wide, 4" deep. *Photo, artist*

Annie Hallam, **Memory.** 2002. Sterling silver formed, fabricated, and etched. The teapot represents the lush and thriving landscape of a farmland from her youth. The intent was to create a design that would embody the sensation of being in a quiet and rural atmosphere. 9.5" high, 8.5" wide, 6" deep. *Photo, artist*

Noël Yovovich, **Just My Cup of Tea** (open, front). Silver, anodized titanium, spinel, glass, copper screen, tourmalines and diamonds. Noël, originally a potter and a jeweler, brought his myriad techniques into play for this unique piece. Five ceramic cups are in the "cabinet." The 6th "pot" is a *trompe l'oeil* teapot, that is actually a flat brooch of gold, anodized titanium, and spinel. It is on a stand, but may be removed and worn. The silver cabinet has glass doors with magnetic closures. On the top is a life-size teabag of copper screen and silver that contains "tea," consisting of fifty carats of mixed tourmaline and over three carats of diamonds. 8" high, 7.5" wide, 2.75" deep. *Photo, Larry Sanders*

Just My Cup of Tea (rear). An intricate interior room scene is etched into the silver showing the china cabinet, but without the spout and handle. It is placed, as it might exist in a house, where one of the teapots has been removed and put to use. *Photo, Larry Sanders*

Valerie Jo Coulson, **The Tempest**. 2002. Constructed in fine and sterling silver with pietersite, poppy jasper, crazy lace agate, obsidian, and tiger's eye. 5.25" high, 4" wide, 2" deep. *Photo, Curtis Haldy*

The Tempest teapot addresses issues and crises that confront us. A prayer niche of a mosque, a rose window, and a cathedral triptych, reference cataclysmic events with factions of the religions. A storm, configured in the pietersite, rains down in dual columns of blood and tears illustrated by the Jasper. The symbology of the spout and handle question the nature of freedom and how it is associated with dependency. A crown of thorns stands in remembrance of innocent victims.

José Chardiet, **Pisa Teapot** (left). 2003. Silver with glass within. 14" high, 9" wide, 2.5" deep. **Wickenden Teapot** (right). 2003. Gold with glass within. 13" high, 7" wide, 2.5" deep. *Courtesy, Habatat Galleries, Chicago, Illinois*

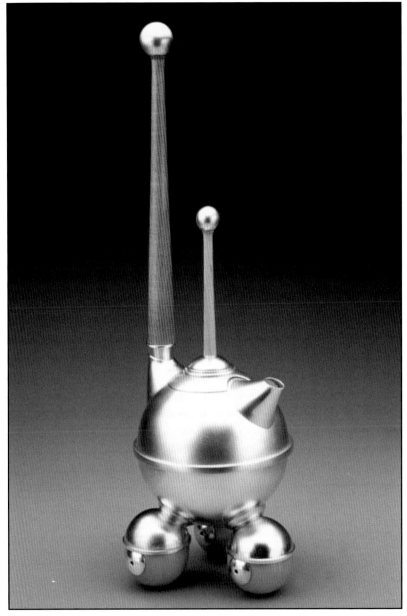

Robin Campo, **Table Tea**. Silver and opal. 4.5" high, 2.5" wide, .05" deep. *Photo, artist*

Wayne S. Sutton, **La Luna Blue**. 1998. Sterling silver with maple handles and wheels. The teapot from a tea set based on the artist's exploration of a circle and a sphere… "the most elegant and beautiful geometric shapes". 16" tall. *Photo, Bill Lemke*

Jennifer L. Monroe, **May I Serve You?** 2002. Sterling silver teapot with the illusion of heat resistant padding, and a pattern. The top lifts out and the thumb is the pouring spout. 9" high, 5" wide, 2.5" deep. *Collection, Gloria and Sonny Kamm. Photo, Jeff Bruce*

Nicole Jacquard, **A Garden of My Own**. 2001. Sterling silver, 18 and 22k gold. The teapot rests in a stand that represents a trellis. When the teapot is removed, a bulb within is in a blossoming stage. 9" high, 4" diam. *Yaw Gallery, Birmingham, Michigan. Photo, Kevin Montague*

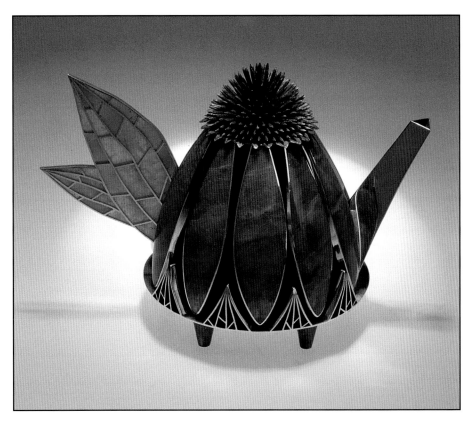

Valerie Jo Coulson, **Echinacea Teapot**. 1998. Sterling silver, with pink rhodonite inlaid in the leaves. The leaves of the handle are inlaid chrysoprases that resemble *pliqué-a-jour* enamel technique. The plant is esteemed for its ability to support the immune system. The relative beauty and symmetry of the blossom reflect the artist's desire to live in concert with nature. 5.5" high, 6" wide, 4" deep. *Photo, Curtis Haldy*

Katherine Ingraham, **Terrace**. Non-functional teapot. Electro-formed fine silver and patina. Patterns, textures, and colors of nature provide the source of inspiration for purely aesthetic reasons and as a record of human energy. 9" high, 7" wide, 5" in. deep. *Collection, Sonny and Gloria Kamm. Mobilia Gallery, Cambridge, Massachusetts. Photo, Dean Powell*

Marilyn da Silva, **Rock, Paper, Scissors Teapot**. 2003. Sterling silver and paint. 10" high, 12" wide, 6" deep. *Mobilia Gallery, Cambridge, Massachusetts. Photo, F. Lee Fatheree*

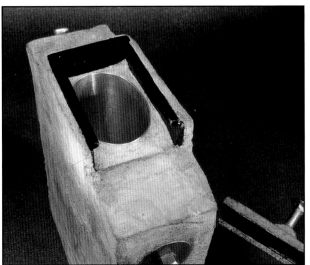

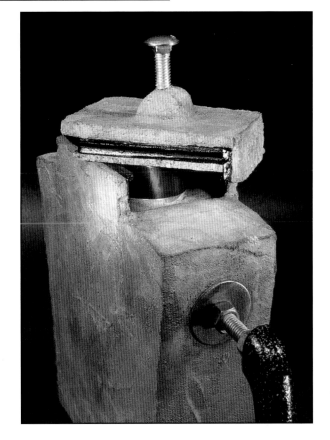

Above:
Charles Lewton-Brain, **Concrete Teapot**. 1993. Sterling silver, wood, polyvinyl cement, expanded polyurethane insulating foam, cork, and steel. The interior is a sterling silver functional pot with a dripless spout. The polyurethane foam helps to keep the tea warm. 11.5" high, 12" wide, 3" deep. *Photo, artist*

Top right:
Charles Lewton-Brain, top view showing the interior silver teapot. *Photo, artist*

Right:
Charles Lewton-Brain, detail of lid assembly and handle. *Photo, artist*

Left:
Penny Michelle, **Teapot Charm Pendants**. Left to right: Classic, Beehive, and Love. Silver and glass. Each silver piece is first made as a wax model, then invested in plaster before lost-wax casting in silver. The glass is a lampworked bead. *Photo, artist*

Bottom left:
Roy, **Rickshaw Teapot Brooch**. 2004. Silver with gold details. The teapot lifts from its base so it can be worn. When not worn it is a sculptural 3-dimensional object that can be turned to "pour," though it is non-functional as a teapot. It combines image and movement; the silver wheel is meant to "transport the viewer to thoughts of the Asian culture". 1.5" high, 4" wide, .75" deep *Photo, artist*

Below:
Tara Summers, **Teapot Pinky Ring**. 2004. Constructed sterling silver. The artist's early exposure to tea parties and afternoon tea with her grandmother made her realize that almost everyone holds out their pinky finger when they drink tea; hence, the idea is appropriate. The spout became the only logical opening for the finger to go through. 1.75" high, 3" wide, 1.5" deep. *Photo, Gary Pollmiller*

Linda Kaye-Moses, **Celestial Traveler's Herbal Tea Locket and Pendant Jewelry**. Front view. Sterling silver, amethyst, and citrine. The selected tea bag scents the surrounding air. The embossed Chinese pictograph represents "earth" and is designed to help keep the wearer's feet planted on our planet. 3" high, 3" wide, .75" deep. *Photo, Evan Soldinger*

Back view with door opened and tea bag inserted. *Photo, Evan Soldinger*

Joan Irvin, **Green Tea and Hibiscus Infusion**. Pendants of sterling silver, anodized aluminum, peridot, and amethyst. Each is 1.5" long, 1" wide. *Photo, artist*

137

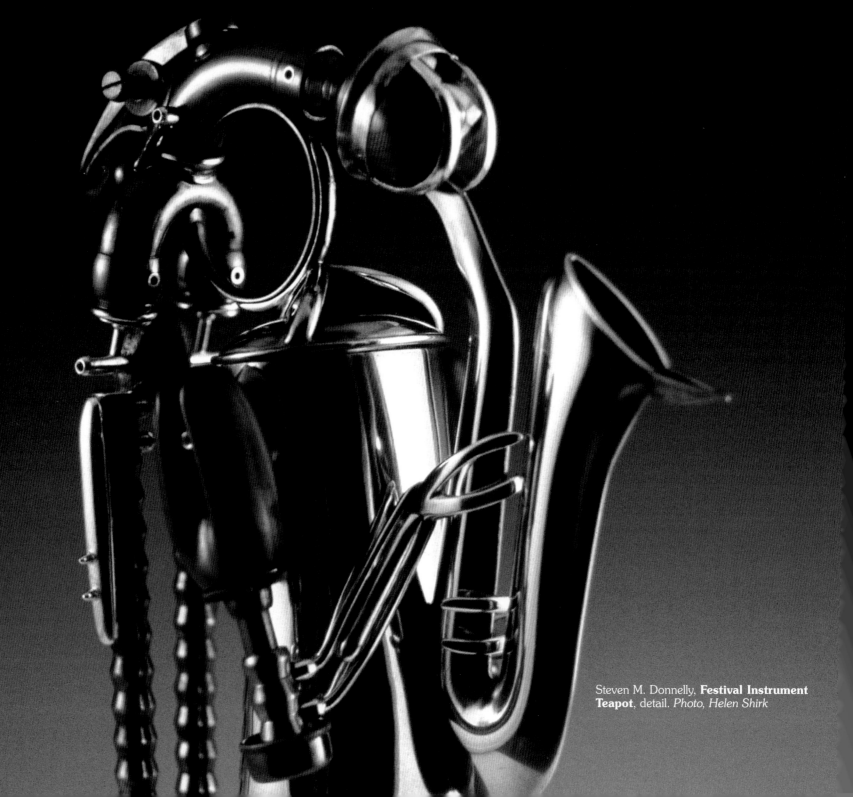

Steven M. Donnelly, **Festival Instrument Teapot**, detail. *Photo, Helen Shirk*

Chapter 6
Mixed Metals and Other Media Teapots

Anyone who has ever eaten in a Chinese restaurant has probably been served tea in a stainless steel teapot. That's true, too, for tea service in many restaurants. Each of these small metal teapots is one of millions manufactured. They are functional, washable, inexpensive, and easily replaced if they become dented or lidless, which is about all a restaurant owner cares about. They have little going for them design wise.

Cast iron teapots, called *tetsubin,* have been manufactured in Japan since about the 17th Century. The Chinese first used cast iron pots for preparing a drink associated with medicinal herbs. When tea brewing and metal pots were brought to Japan, they developed the *tetsubin* teapot. They were used for centuries to heat water over open fires for ceremonies. Cast iron stays hot even longer than porcelain, and most *tetsubin* pots have an enamel interior that's easy to clean. If the enamel chips, however, the inside of the pot can rust.

Tetsubin are cast from molds so that many copies of a single design can be made. The casting process also enables an artisan to create intricate designs in the mold and many *tetsubin* often have dragons, lotus flowers, leaves, and other symbolic images. Usually, the pots are small, round, and flattened from top to bottom. They are not used in the traditional Japanese tea ceremony.

The one-of-a-kind artist-made metal teapots in this chapter may be functional, but more likely they are not. As with ceramics, they become a sculptural form that expresses the artists' reactions to life and the world. The following explanations emphasize that perception.

Steven M. Donnelly's *Festival Instrument* teapot was conceived as a commemorative piece in celebration of the new millennium. Symbolically, teapots can embody the concepts of ritual and service as the tea is poured to fill cups of those present. Donnelly says, "My idea began as a musical notion and, because festivals are a common form of celebration in every culture, the theme is particularly apt. Musicians at a festival are much like the ritual tea service. The musician pours music from his instrument and joins those gathered. The

teapot is a gesture of optimism and hope for the world; and an homage to the music and musicians that unite us at times of festivals and celebrations."

Curtis H. Arima bases his teapot designs on the human body along with plant and related forms. The objects borrow from reality and mutate into dreamlike objects. All metal work is raised, forged, and fabricated. No parts are cast.

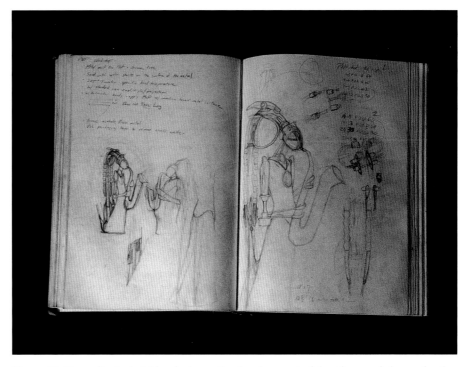

Steven M. Donnelly. A sketchbook shows the development of the ideas and shapes for the **Festival Instrument Teapot**. *Photo, Helen Shirk*

Some pieces integrate clay with the metal. Color is achieved from the first heat on the metal and/or by adding a liver of sulfur patina, followed by anywhere from 10 to 40 layers of acrylic washes.

There are many techniques for working metal and the more one knows, the more versatile they become. Jon M. Route's demonstration of a few techniques, and the teapots that follow, will help you understand how much metallurgical knowledge is needed and how varied a teapot can be in overall design, surface treatment, colors, and combinations of different metals, and media.

The concept of mixed materials opens up a whole bag of exciting prospects. Peter Shire isn't the least bashful or traditional about materials he combines. His mixed media teapots barely resemble the teapot form; rather they can be considered assemblages using any parts he may decide go together.

Lindsay Rais shapes her teapot body of stainless steel mesh. She adds knotless netting procedures for fashioning the lid, sewing with silver and copper coated wire, then making a base of pistachio nut shells. Mary Chuduk also uses copper screen; she colors areas with enamel for her see- through teapot.

Jean Neeman mixes metals with Lucite. Michael Jerry uses metal raising techniques for his teapots and adds wood handles he carves himself. John Rais and Susan Madacsi use the blacksmith's techniques of forging and shaping hot iron to create their teapots.

Harriete Estel Berman brings a unique originality to her materials and how she uses them, along with an uncanny design sense. There's no money invested in basic materials, just a lot of finding and gathering tins from products such as cookies, tea, popcorn cans, and more, and more. The witty, thought provoking objects she makes from these recycled tins have become her signature. They also make a statement against waste.

Berman's work may include techniques used for fine silversmithing such as raising, forging, and construction. She wonders, does a piece have value because of the materials? By how it is made? Or by who made it? In her case, trash is transformed into objects of value that are quickly bought up.

You will also have the opportunity to think about how the world looks through teapot shaped glasses, especially if you have a pair of Charli Verga's *Tea Time Glasses*. Wear them with I-Ling Chen's *Copper Teapot Necklace* and your teapot shopping forays will be a source of interest and amusement to everyone who sees you.

Tetsubin Tea Kettle. Cast iron with a bamboo design and a stainless steel mesh infuser. A tea kettle holds 20 ounces, a smaller teapot holds only about 6 ounces. *Private collection. Photo, Dona Meilach*

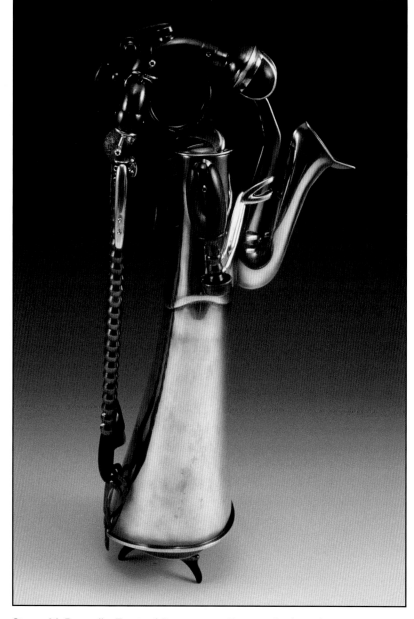

Steven M. Donnelly, **Festival Instrument Teapot**. Sterling silver, antique coronet parts, brass hardware, bronze, copper, canarywood, and ebony. Integrating antique coronet parts required a complex set of cold connections because of the horn's original fabrication with a lead based, low temperature solder. 11" high, 4" wide, 5" deep. *Photo, Helen Shirk*

John M. Route, **Curley-Top Teapot**. 2000. Pewter, brass, and copper. 6.5" high, 4" wide, 2.5" deep. *del Mano Gallery, Los Angeles, California. Photo, Deborah Route*

Jon M. Route, **Copperberry Teapot**. Jon Route uses a variety of metalworking tools and techniques to create his copper teapots. 10" high, 11" wide, 6" deep. *Photo, Deborah Route*

Right:
Jon M. Route uses an H-frame hydraulic press to apply a fold-forming technique that creates lines or creases for the pattern that will be the teapot body. The 16-gauge pewter was first textured with a rubber mallet on a rough piece of concrete.

After creating and texturing the body pattern, the pewter is flattened, then formed into a cone shape by hand. The ends must meet contiguously and on the same plane. Then the metal is fused, or welded, together with an acetylene torch.

Right:
After fusing, the piece is hammered so that the seam literally disappears. The whole shape is planished on a blow-horn stake to achieve a consistent form and surface. *Photo series, Deborah Route.*

Jon M. Route, **Patchwork Leaf Teapot**.
1999. Pewter, brass, and copper. 13" high,
11" wide, 4" deep. *del Mano Gallery, Los
Angeles, California. Photo, Deborah
Route*

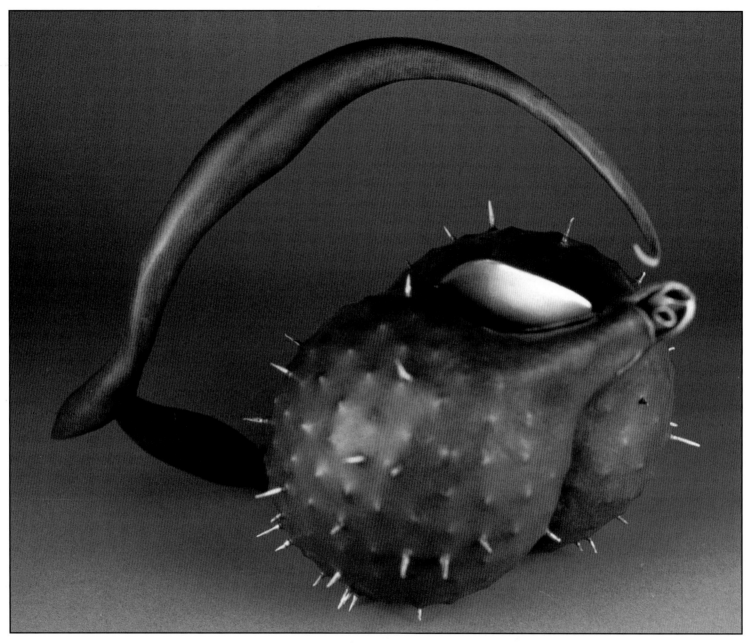

Curtis H. Arima, **Broken Propagation Teapot**. 2003. Copper, sterling silver, and acrylics. The nature of plant propagation sometimes goes awry. The imagery reflects the elements of propagation; earth, water, and plant parts. 9" high, 18" wide, 10" deep. *Mobilia Galleria, Cambridge, Massachusetts. Photo, artist*

Curtis H. Arima, **Teapot.** 1998. Copper, sterling silver, and acrylic. The main body of the teapot is raised from two sheets of metal and the handle is spiculum formed. 10" high, 9" long, 8" wide. *Mobilia Gallery, Cambridge, Massachusetts. Photo, Steve Selvin*

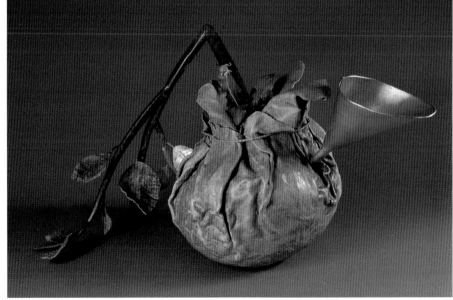

Curtis H. Arima, **Bladed Ball and Socket Teapot**. 1999. The main body is clay with steel spikes. The handle is copper with a movable ball-joint and a nickel blade. Acrylic color washes are used on the surfaces. 9" high, 12" wide, 16" deep. *Photo, artist*

Opposite page:
Katherine A. Ingraham, **Tonic**. From "Here's to Your Health" series. Electroformed copper and enamel. 7.5" high, 10" wide, 6" deep. *Collection, Gloria and Sonny Kamm. Mobilia Gallery, Cambridge, Massachusetts. Photo, Dean Powell*

Opposite page(inset):
Katherine A. Ingraham, **Tonic**. A bird's eye view looking into the pot shows the precise construction of the copper woven around the spokes. *Photo, Dean Powell*

Left:
Wayne S. Sutton, **Harvest**. 1996. Copper, sterling silver, wood, straw, aluminum, and oil and water base paint. 10" high, 7" wide, 4.5" deep. *Photo, artist*

Agnes Pal, **Adolph's Playground, II**. Copper and patina. The forms hearken back to her childhood, when there were only thistles to play with in a German concentration camp. 14" high, 8" wide. *Photo, Jeff Bruce*

Agnes Pal, **Adolph's Playground**. Copper with patina. 14" high, 12" deep. *Photo, Jeff Bruce*

David Huang, **Red Tea #300**. Copper, sterling silver, and 23k gold leaf. 4" high, 6.25" wide, 4.5" deep. *Courtesy, del Mano Gallery, Los Angeles, California. Photo, David Peters©2004*

Marilyn da Silva, **Harlequin**. One of a pair. 1998. Copper, brass, gold plate, gesso, and colored pencil. Each is 4" high 6" wide, 3" deep. *Photo, M. Lee Fatherree*

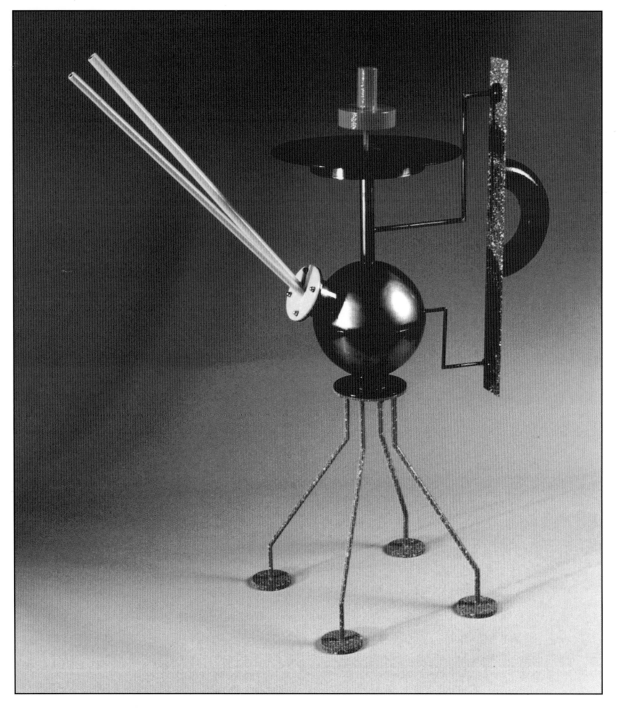

Peter Shire, **Torso Split**. 1993. Steel, polyester, and enamel. 31" high, 26.5" wide, 11" deep. *Photo, William Nettles*

Peter Shire, **Sapporo**. 1994. Steel, aluminum, branch, polyester, and enamel. 26" high, 26" wide, 10" deep. *Photo, William Nettles*

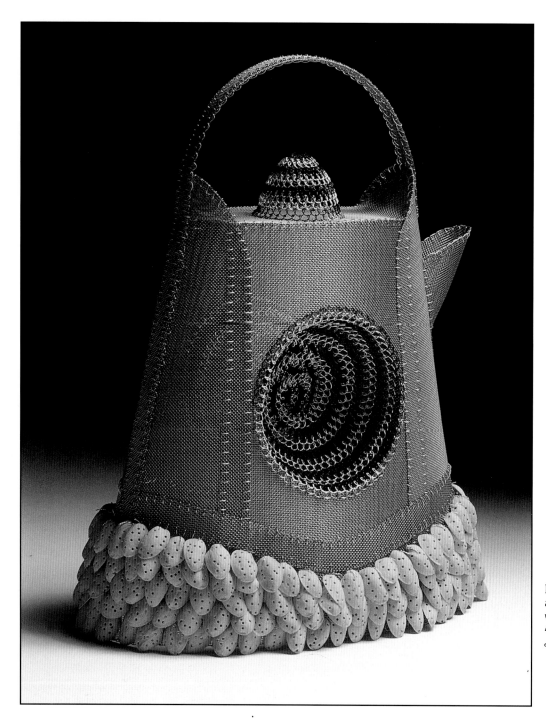

Lindsay K. Rais, **Teapot**. 2003. Stainless steel mesh, anti-tarnish silver, and coated copper knotless netting, with pistachio nutshells at the base. 12.5" high, 10" wide, 4" deep. *Collection, Gloria and Sonny Kamm. Photo, D. James Dee*

Michael Jerry, **Ruffle Pot**. Pewter with cherry handles. 7.5" high, 10" wide. *Patina Gallery, Santa Fe, New Mexico. Photo, artist*

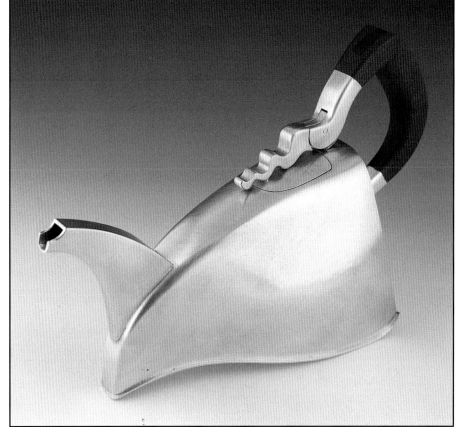

Michael Jerry, **TeaPot**. Pewter with cherry handle. 7.5" high, 7.25" wide. *Patina Gallery, Santa Fe, New Mexico. Photo, artist*

Jean Neeman, **Heart's Delight**. 1992. Copper, brass, nickel, and acrylics. 5.75" high, 8.24" wide, 3.5" deep. *Collection, Gloria and Sonny Kamm. Photo, Tony Cunha*

Linda Weiss, **Teapot**. Patinated copper, silver plated interior, ebony handle, and Picasso marble finial. 9.5" high, 5.5" wide, 7" deep. *Photo, artist*

John Rais, **Swollen Chamber**. 2003. Hollow formed & forged steel with a patina. *Collection, Gloria and Sonny Kamm. Photo, D. James Dee*

Susan Madacsi, **Teapot with Cup**. Forged sheet steel. The color and patterns are from stenciling with enamel paints. Teapot: 5.5" high, 9.5" long, 4" wide. Cup: 3" high, 2.5" long, 1" wide. *Photo, R.J. Philt*

David Gignac, **Three Stage**. 2001. Forged and fabricated steel. 27.5" high, 25" wide, 6.25" deep. *Collection, Gloria and Sonny Kamm. Photo, Tony Cunha*

Jack da Silva, detail of the bottom front. "Faith, Hope, and Love, the greatest of these is Love." This teapot focuses on life's travails and where we ultimately find comfort. Using Braille raised letters, "Faith" appears in the upper ring. "Hope" is on the lower ring, and "Love" is on the main vessel with the corks held in place using glass-head quilting pins. *Photo, M. Lee Fatherree*

Jack da Silva, **The Greatest of These: Drawn to Believe**. 2003. Sterling silver, lumber pencils, stainless steel, nylon, cork, and glass head quilter pins. 8" high, 6" wide, 2" deep. *Photo, M. Lee Fatherree*

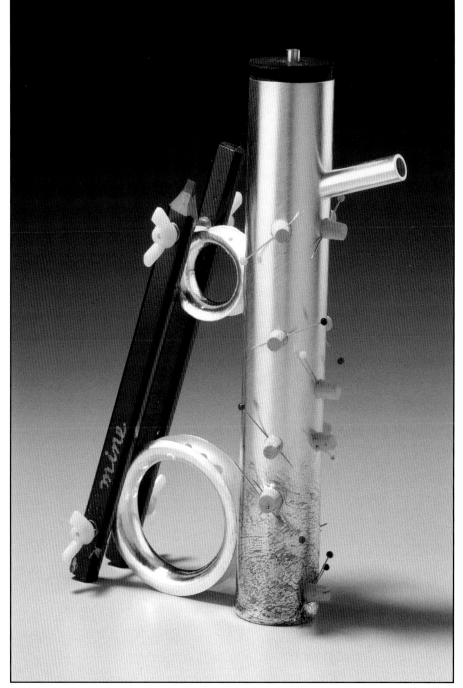

Mike Edelman, **Chain Maile Teapot**. Stainless steel rings hand coiled, cut, and woven. No reinforcements were used to hold the shape. Chain weaves used for armor and jewelry gave the piece the necessary tension so it would not flop around. 6" high, 7.5" long, 5" wide. *Collection, Gloria and Sonny Kamm. Photo, artist*

Mary Chuduk, **Tea Strainer.** 2003. Enamel on copper screen. Experimenting with alternative materials led her to testing the flexibility of copper screen for sculptural forms. The idea of a teapot that could be the strainer was a tongue-in-cheek approach to creating the form. 8.5" high, 11" wide, 5" deep. *Photo, Jeff Scovil*

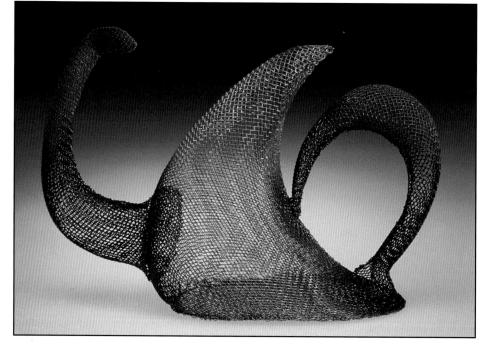

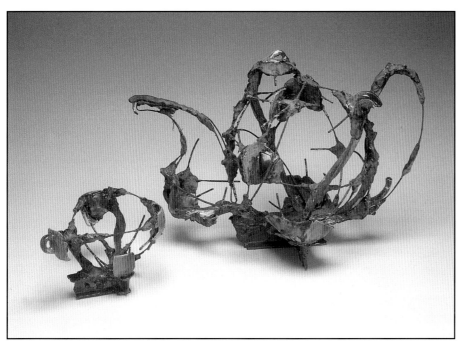

Raymon Elozua, **Wire Frame Teapot #3 with cup**. 1992. Steel frame with terra-cotta, and glaze. Teapot: 19.5" high, 27" wide, 15" deep. Cup: 7.25" high, 11.5" wide, 10.25" deep. *Collection, Gloria and Sonny Kamm. Photo, Tony Cunha*

Linda Threadgill, **Forsaking Ornament**. 2002. Bronze, micarta and resin. The resin is cast and etched. Teapot is 14" high, 12" wide, 5" deep. The tray is 1.6" high, 13" wide. *Collection, Gloria and Sonny Kamm. Courtesy, Mobilia Gallery, Cambridge, Massachusetts*

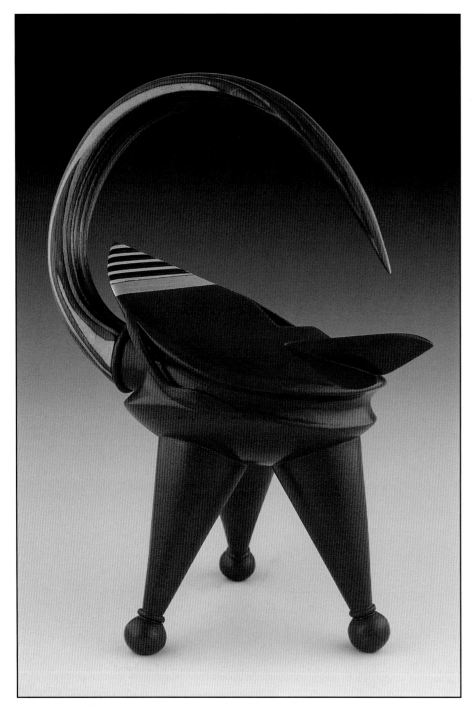

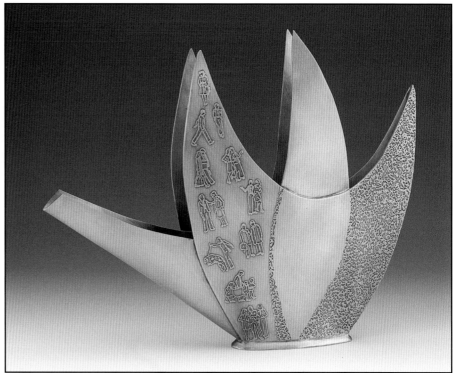

Claire Pfleger, **Teapot**. Pewter. Based on the idea of a flower opening. 5.5" high, 6.5" wide. *Photo, Larry Sanders*

Wayne S. Sutton, **Retrograde Red**. 2003. Pewter, laminated Baltic birch with pigment and enamel paint. 9" high. *Photo, artist*

Deborah Lozier, **Teapot Kimono**. 2000. Copper and enamel. This bottomless teapot was made from one piece of copper cut from a pattern as one would make in dressmaking. There is only one long welded seam at the handle and a long fold at the spout. The etched design on the pot is from a Japanese color stencil for paper. The enameling technique is torch-fired champlevé. 7.5" high, 6.5" wide, 4" deep. *Photo, artist*

Marilyn Moore, **Tea Squared**. 2002. Stitched copper wire cloth with copper wire. 10" high, 10" wide, 5.25" deep. *Photo, Jerry McCollum*

Helen Shirk, **Orange Plume Teapo**t. 2001. Copper, patina, and colored pencils. 13" high, 11" wide, 4" deep. *Photo, artist*

Helen Shirk, **Blue Grass Teapot**. 2003. Copper, patina, and colored pencils. 10" tall, 9" wide, 5.5" deep. *Photo, artist*

Marilyn da Silva, **An Unlikely Pair**. 1998. Copper, brass, gold plate, gesso, and colored pencil. 4" high, 6" wide, 3" deep.
Photo, M. Lee Fatherree

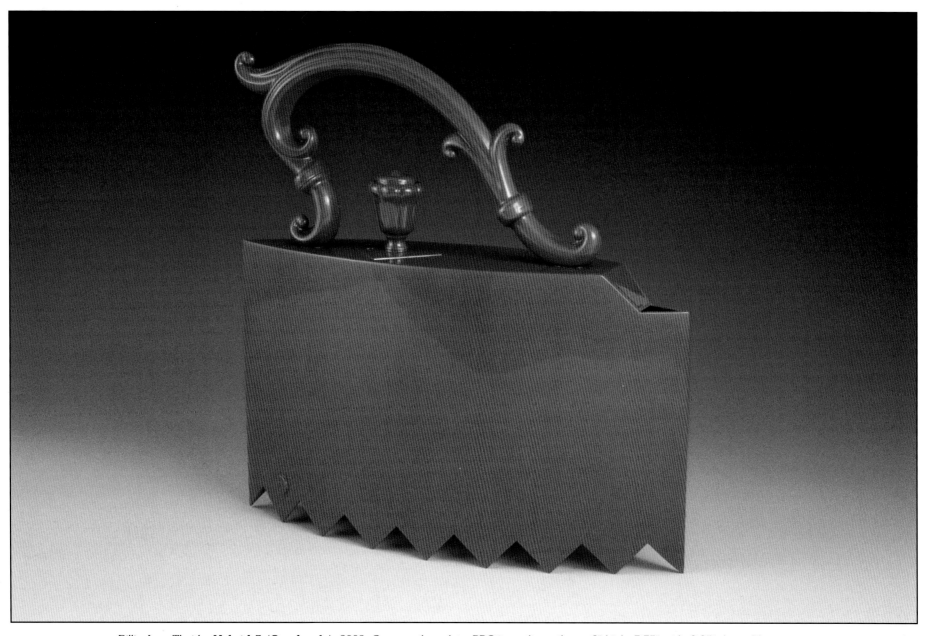

Billie Jean Theide, **Hybrid 5 (Quadruple)**. 2003. Copper, silver plate, PPG® acrylic urethane. 8" high, 7.75" wide 2.25" deep. *Photo, artist*

Billie Jean Theide, **Hybrid 3 (VanBergh)**. 2001. Copper, silver plate, PPG® acrylic urethane. 7" high, 9" wide, 2.5" deep. *Photo, artist*

Harriete Estel Berman at work in her studio. Her "storehouse" of materials may appear chaotic, but her found tin materials are carefully sortedby color and subject. Amid thousands of pieces of "recycleable" tin, she can find what she needs for a special idea almost instantly. All pieces shown, Collection, *Gloria and Sonny Kamm. Courtesy, artist*

After her idea has germinated, she makes a paper template before cutting the tin into shapes. *Photo, artist*

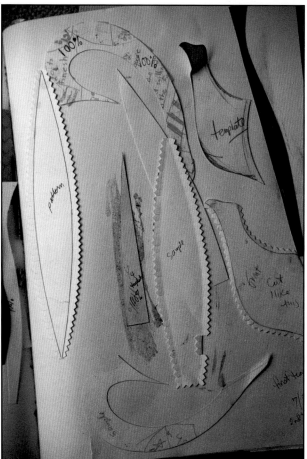

Harriete Estel Berman, **Consuming Good Taste**. 1999. Teapot with stand. The teapot is made from pre-printed tin containers and joined with aluminum and brass rivets. Images have been altered from a famous painting reproduced to sell consumer products. 11" high, 11.5" wide. *Mobilia Gallery, Cambridge, Massachusetts. Photo, Philip Cohn*

Harriete Estel Berman, **Bittersweet Obsession**. 2003. Chocolate pot and four cups constructed from pre-printed steel from recycled tin containers. There are also 10k gold, aluminum rivets, and brass and stainless steel screws. 20" high, 15.5" wide, 6.5" deep. *Photo, Philip Cohn*

Left:
Harriete Estel Berman, **Coffee Pot: The Golden Ratio**. Constructed from pre-printed steel from recycled tin containers for ILLY coffee, 10K gold, and aluminum rivets, and stainless steel screws. The stacked espresso cups are permanently attached with a concealed rod through their centers. The coffeepot shape is based on a historical coffeepot from 1728-1729. The ratio for the height of the pot to the height of the precariously stacked espresso cups is based on the concept of *phi* (pronounced 'fee'), The Golden Ratio, and a pun on the word on "coffee". Would you like milk and sugar with your coffee? 22" high, 12" wide, 6.25" deep. *Photo, Philip Cohn*

167

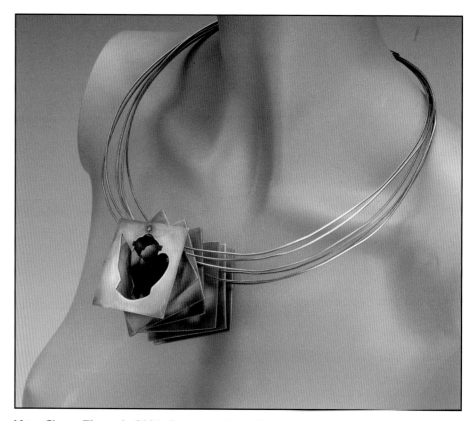

I-Ling Cheng, **Through**. 2004. Copper necklace. Pierced and constructed. 9.5" high, 7.5" wide, 3" deep. *Photo, Gary Pollmiller*

Joan Irvin, **Holly Teapot**. Foil, brass, copper, steel, and a neck hoop of anodized aluminum. 2.25" high, 1.5" wide on a 5" diam. hoop. *Photo, artist*

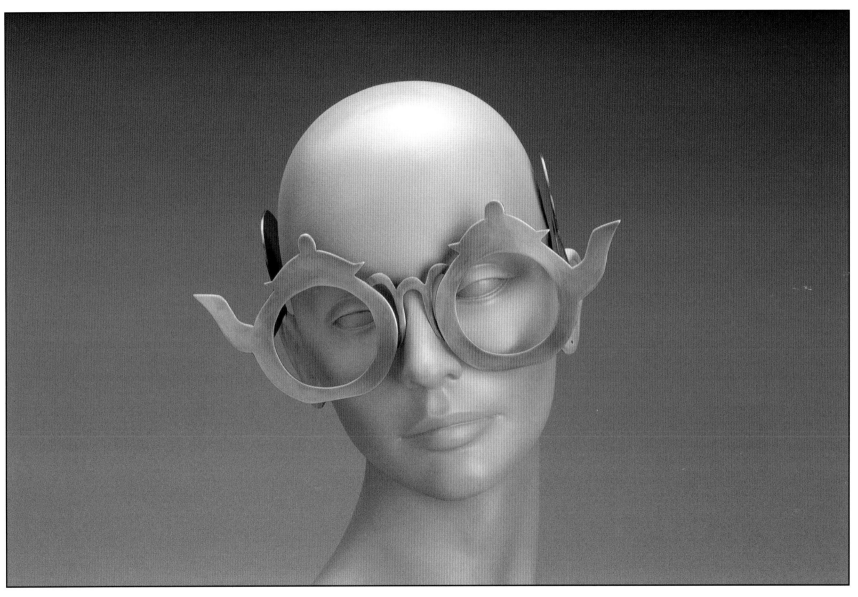

Charli Verga, **Teatime Specs**. 2004. Constructed copper. 3.5" high, 8.25" wide, 6" deep. *Photo, Gary Pollmiller*

Garry Cohen, **Rooster Teapot Series**. Hen and two chickens are made using the hot blown glass technique. That means the piece is totally made by hot blowing as opposed to pieces with parts blown separately, and then assembled with glues. 12" to 14" tall. *Photo, Dona Meilach*

170

Chapter 7

Glass Teapots

The potential of glass as a medium with expressive and versatile properties is being explored by more and more studio artists. Glass can be thin or thick, transparent or opaque, plain or magnificently colored. It can be cut, carved, etched, sand blasted, and sanded like wood. When it is molten, it is movable and malleable like hot iron. Blowing into hot glass can expand it. It can be cast like bronze, and constructed like found objects. Colors can be added while it is being blown. After it has hardened, colors can be adding by fusing.

Core-formed and cast glass vessels were first produced in Egypt and Mesopotamia as early as the fifteenth century B.C., but only began to be imported and made on the Italian peninsula in the mid-first millennium B.C. By the time of the Roman Republic (509–27 B.C.), such vessels, used as tableware or as containers for expensive oils, perfumes, and medicines, were common in Italy.

Roman artisans proved their versatility with glassblowing by 150 B.C. Free form shapes were made by blowing the hot glass into the open air. Other shapes were the result of contouring the hot, soft glass with ceramic or metal tools. Another technique involved blowing the glass into shaped molds so that the resulting bubble deformed and replicated the mold's interior. This method of glass molding opened a wide range of creative opportunities. Elaborate scenes were often engraved inside the molds that transferred to the glass and produced an embossed surface. Engraving was also accomplished by working the hard glass with tools just as one would engrave wood.

Pyrex glass teapots were manufactured shortly after World War 1. Corning Glass had developed a heat-resistant and stronger glass that could withstand sudden temperature changes for lantern globes, scientific, and medical research purposes. Early Pyrex teapots were purely functional with unembellished straightforward designs.

The pioneers of modern art glass, Louis Tiffany, René Lalique, and Émile Gallé, used commercial equipment in glass factories during the Art Nouveau period, around 1900, and were the first artists to sign their work. Today's artists who work with art glass owe their gratitude to four men who began creating glass as art in the early 1960s, when they discovered that glass could be melted at temperatures low enough to permit the use of a small furnace.

Harvey Littleton, a professor of fine arts at the University of Wisconsin, and Dominick Labino, a physicist, realized that a small furnace could be set up in a home, a backyard, an art school, a museum, almost anywhere. They completely redirected the future for art glass and it had an international impact.

In 1966, Dale Chihuly studied glassblowing under Harvey Littleton and he blew away any preconceptions about what art glass should be. Chihuly's output and influence today are undisputed and artists who attended workshops at his school in Pilchuck, Washington, have accomplished much of the art glass one sees. His influence has made Seattle, Washington, the acknowledged center of the modern art glass movement.

Richard Marquis has also had an extraordinary influence on the development of contemporary studio glass in America and around the world. Studying at the University of California at Berkeley during the 1960s, he explored ceramics and was introduced to glassblowing. His investigation of the potential of glass took him to the island of Murano, near Venice, to observe and work with the masters of the Venetian glassblowing tradition. Through teaching and demonstrations, his influence on a generation of artists has led to the redefinition of glass as an artistic medium. His teapots are exquisitely colored and shaped.

Glass today is a major art medium in the form of sculpture, jewelry, windows, hangings, and, of course, vessels. That nomenclature has spilled over into a fascination with artist-made glass teapots that are on the cutting edge of valuable art collectibles.

Garry Cohen, who teaches glass art at a southern California college, has built a glass studio on his property in Escondido, California. Watching him create his chicken and rooster shaped teapots is like watching dancers perform; in fact the area surrounding his workbench is referred to as "the dance floor."

An assistant gathers the glass colorants on a heated punty rod or a blow pipe, walks it to the furnace, and puts it into the "glory hole." When it is heated to a near viscous state, the assistant walks the pipe to Garry's workbench. Slowly, carefully Garry begins to blow through the blow pipe, to generate a bubble that becomes the chicken's body. Then swiftly, deftly he shapes the bubble into the form he wants, constantly twirling the pipe so the shape doesn't droop. When it air cools and hardens to a stiffness he can no longer manipulate, the assistant returns it to the glory hole to reheat.

During the shaping process, and as the chicken form builds, the assistant moves back and forth with additional molten glass and new colors. It's a constant back and forth display that is as rhythmic as a dance.

In addition to blown glass, examples that follow include glass that is sewn, cast, fused, enameled, and flame worked.

Garry Cohen Creates a Glass Rooster Teapot

Garry Cohen demonstrates the creation of his rooster and chicken teapots at his glass studio. The entire process must be done quickly as the glass is heated and cools, heated and cools several times. Making this one teapot required about an hour of intense concentration, a quick and sure technique, and the help of an efficient assistant.

1. Garry Cohen's raw coloring materials for glass blowing include different types and grades of rods, frit or sand, and powder. *Photo, series, Dona Meilach*

2. Garry's assistant has picked up colorant on a blowpipe end. He inserts the pipe end into the glory hole (lehr or oven) and heats it until the glass becomes molten and malleable.

3. Garry blows into the blowpipe to puff up a shape for the rooster's body, always turning and manipulating the pipe as he works.

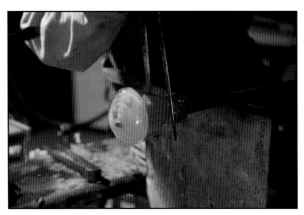

4. He continues to shape the vessel and creates a crack-off line for turning. The material is reheated so it can continue to be turned and shaped.

5. The rooster's foot is picked up and shaped. The piece will be transferred from the blow pipe to a punting rod so the head end can be developed. First it must be reheated in the glory hole.

172

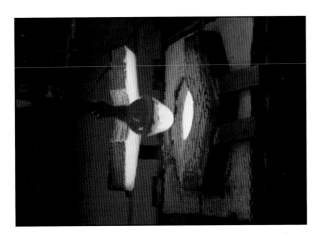

6. After forming the body, the piece is rolled into a colored powder or a glob of colored glass, reheated and applied to the rooster in select areas.

7. Additional glass will become the bottom part of the lid. Excess glass is nipped off.

8. Shaping the head end continues by holding wet papers and shaping tools against the spinning hot glass.

9. The black and white finial that serves as the rooster's "comb" is added. It matches the lid's base.

Final detailing before finishing. The finished piece must be placed in a cooling oven for 24 hours to bring the entire object to the same temperature. The gradual cooling prevents the glass from cracking or breaking.

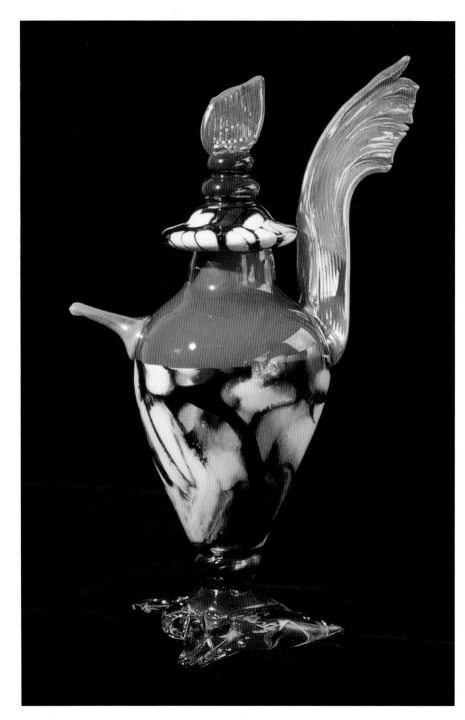

Garry Cohen holds another of his finished roosters. Each has a different color scheme. These teapots are not functional; they are sculptural and illustrate the potential of glass for artistic teapot forms.

Garry Cohen, The finished rooster.

Miia Virtasalmi picks up a glass bubble from the glory hole of the kiln for one element in her teapot sculpture. *Photo, Robert Tannahill*

Miia Virtasalmi, **Something to Drink?** 1999.
Glass and high-fired enamel. 22.5" high, 10.6"
wide, 8.6" deep. *Photo, artist*

Above:
Gavin Heath, **Teapots**. Blown glass and painted. Heath, raised in South Africa, brings the colors and culture of his native country to his brightly painted fantasy works. *Photo, Rick Lang*

Left:
Miia Virtasalmi, **Last Piece of Cake**. Blown glass and high-fired enamels. Teapot from a larger installation consisting of glass bubbles with painted faces of "guests." The teapot with the image at left shows the last piece of cake in the hand of a guest. *Photo, artist*

Opposite page:
Gavin Heath. **Teapots**. Blown glass and painted. Creativity shows spirit, which is of no particular religion or ideal. *Photo, Rick Lang*

Tim Drier, **Blue and Red Striped Pot**. Flameworked borosilicate (Pyrex) Glass. 10" high, 8" wide, 4" deep. *Photo, Jeff Glenn*

Tim Drier, **Pollen #2**. Flameworked borosilicate (Pyrex) glass. 8" high, 8" wide, 4" deep. *Photo, Jeff Glenn*

Tim Drier's Flameworked Glass

Tim Drier is intrigued with the human body and its unparalleled complexity. His hollow forms are enriched with hints of color. Each teapot is created over a propane bench burner, (dubbed Flamework) and the partially melted borosilicate (Pyrex) glass is painstakingly shaped by pushing and pulling as it is heated. Flameworked glass is a hobby for Drier, whose continuing profession is in scientific glassblowing where he designs and creates glassware for research and industrial chemical endeavors. For his flameworked teapots, he often looks to Venetian and Art-Nouveau styles and imbues each of his pieces with clean lines and a sensual simplicity.

Tim Drier, **Man Handle**. Flameworked borosilicate (Pyrex) Glass. 10" high, 8" wide, 4" deep. *Photo, Jeff Glenn*

Susan Glasgow's Sewn Glass Teapots

Susan Taylor Glasgow's techniques for sewing glass are a personal discovery based on her experience as a seamstress. She says, "My work is the result of homemaking skills gone awry. My life as an artist puts housekeeping last while instead, I cook, arrange, and sew glass. My internal domestic struggle has led me to examine the concept of domestic expectations and traditional roles of men and women. I am intrigued by 1950s imagery and the false perception of simpler times. My work combines the domestic act of sewing with nostalgic imagery to create pieces that hint at complex expectations behind closed doors."

Susan Taylor Glasgow, **Sewing Susan Contemplates Running with Scissors**. Glass fused, draped, sandblasted, enameled, and stitched with waxed linen thread. 2002 Niche Award winner. 9.5" high, 9" wide, 6" deep. *Photo, artist*

Susan Taylor Glasgow, **Atomic Teapot**. Sewn glass panels fused, draped, sand-blasted, enameled, stitched with waxed linen thread, and buttons. 9.5" high, 9" wide. *Photo, artist*

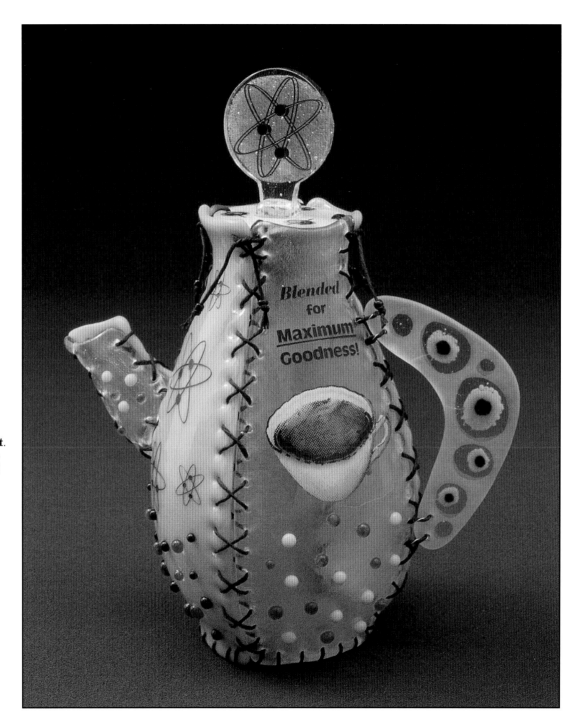

The technical process of creating and sewing glass panels together is a time consuming labor of love. Each teapot sculpture or vessel starts out as a flat sheet of glass. Each section of glass is kiln-fired several times to establish the three-dimensional shape and holes.

To create the imagery, the text and figures are sandblasted into the glass, and pigment is rubbed into the sandblasted area to achieve the black and gray "photo." The components are then re-fired at 1250° Fahrenheit to melt the pigment into the glass. Once cooled, the sections are cold-worked, sandblasted again, and assembled. Depending on the complexity of the piece, the entire creative process takes approximately two to four weeks to complete.

Susan Taylor Glasgow, **Act Like A Lady Teapot Book**. 2004. Glass. 20" high, 20" wide, 7" deep. *Collection, Gloria and Sonny Kamm. Photos, artist*

182

Susan Taylor Glasgow in her workshop preparing to cut a piece of glass. Several types of equipment are required for the many procedures involved.

Susan cuts the glass using the template for her pattern.

Susan Taylor Glasgow, (detail).

She places the panels and other parts in the kiln.

Coloring a Glass Mold with *Pâte de Verre*

Steve Linn makes his forms in a mold and colors them using the *pâte de verre* method. *Pâte de verre* involves creating a paste from colored frit (small particles of glass). The paste is applied to the surface of the mold, and then the mold and its contents are fired in a kiln. *Pâte de verre* allows for precise placement of particular glass colors in the mold. Other ways of filling the mold often result in some shifting of glass from where it has been placed before firing, but the *pâte de verre* process helps control this shifting.

Pâte de verre dates back to the ancient Egyptians. It was popularized again about a century ago by a group of French artists who revived it, and gave the technique its current name. In traditional French *pâte de verre*, the artist mixed crushed glass with enamels or paint to form a paste that was carefully placed in a mold and then fired. Many of the pieces that were made using this technique were relatively small, elaborately decorated, and required more than one firing before they were complete.

Steve Linn, **Bizarre Ware: Homage to Clarice Cliff**. *Pâte de verre* molded glass teapots with cast bronze plant forms. *Pâte de verre* involves creating a mold for the glass shape. Colored paste is added in specific areas of the kiln. The glass and mold are fired in the kiln and the color remains on the glass piece. 25.2" high, 23.6" wide, 21.6" deep. *Collection, Gloria and Sonny Kamm. Habatat Gallery, Royal Oak, Michigan. Photo, artist*

Hugh E. McKay, **T-pot**. 2003. Cast
leaded glass by the lost wax technique. This
piece was first made in wood, then molds made
and the glass was cast. 11" high, 11" wide, 7"
deep. *Photo, artist*

David Gignac, **Delivery**. Blown glass, oil paint, forged and fabricated steel.
24" high, 8" wide, 5" deep. *Collection, Gloria and Sonny Kamm. Courtesy,
Ferrin Gallery, Lenox, Massachusetts*

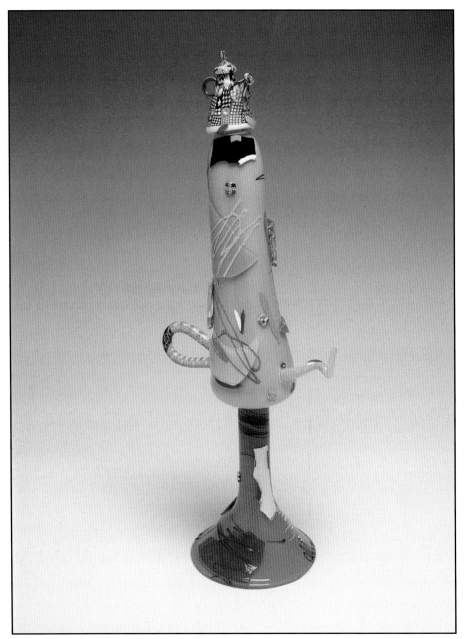

Richard Marquis, **Teapot and Trophy**. 1990. Blown glass, Murrine technique, zanfirico rod handles, and paint. Marquis is often referred to as the "king" of blown glass teapots. 28" high, 11.5" wide, 7.5" deep. *Collection, Gloria and Sonny Kamm. Photo, Tony Cunha*

Richard Marquis, **Teapot Goblet**. 1988. Blown glass with zanfirico technique. 9.5" high, 3.5" diam. Collection, *Gloria and Sonny Kamm. Photo, Tony Cunha*

Alison Sheafor, **Wacky Teapot Necklace**. 1996. Eighteen glass teapots. Blown glass. Each teapot is small and requires extremely deft handling of the blow pipe and colored glass additions. 30" long. *Collection, Gloria and Sonny Kamm. Photo, Tony Cunha*

Richard Marquis, **Teapot Goblet**. 1991. Zanfirico technique. 10.5" high, 4.75" wide, 3.5" deep. *Collection, Gloria and Sonny Kamm. Photo, Tony Cunha*

Christian H. Thirion's pieces explode with color, figuratively. He says, "My teapots are a riot of color. I have to feel good about the colors fitting together along with the movement of the piece. I love to bring an element of whimsy into my work." *Photo, artist*

Christian H. Thirion, **Glass Teapot**. This piece earned the Niche Award at the *2003 Rozen Buyers Market of American Craft.* It consists of a blown teapot with a little teapot inside. All pieces are made together hot, there is no gluing involved, so technically, it was a very difficult piece to make. 12" high, 10" wide, 6" deep. *Photo, artist*

Christian H. Thirion, **Crazy Teapot With Cup**. 12" high, 10" wide, 6" deep. *Photo, artist*   Christian H. Thirion, **Crazy Teapot**. 12" high, 10" wide, 6" deep. *Photo, artist*

Constance Roberts, **Ark Tea Set**. 1995. Wood. Hand carved and painted. There are 28 animals in the ark and each is a whistle. 10" high, 14" wide, 10" deep. Collection, Gloria and Sonny Kamm. Photo, Tony Cunha

Chapter 8
Trees and Plants, Wood and Paper

Can you imagine teapots made of wood? Of paper? How could they function as teapots? Why would artists make them? Why would people collect them?

The answers are both simple and complex. There is no question that wood or paper teapots cannot function as vessels for holding water or making tea. However, they can function as a challenging sculptural medium for creating a form that intrigues artists. If artists make them, there are bound to be collectors who want them. If collectors want them, artists will add them to their output.

Yes. Many people collect teapots to display and not to use. Is there any reason why a sculpture should not be in the shape of a teapot any more than one might be in the shape of a shoe that can't be worn, a hat that can't protect the head? Or even an oversized metal clothespin or other ordinary item such as those made by Claes Oldenburg? They have no practical function. They are an expressive art form to be displayed, enjoyed, talked about and, perhaps stir up conversation and controversy.

Animals, two of a kind, surround Constance Roberts' wooden hand carved teapot in the form of Noah's Ark as if waiting to board. The dish, encircled by a rainbow rim might symbolize the waters around Mt. Ararat at Dogubayazit, Turkey. It is symbolic, it tells a story, but it is a sculpture, pure and simple. Wood carving and wood working techniques are used and the rendition would probably produce a smile from most people.

Gina Freuen chose to make her rendition of a teapot a stylized drawing on paper. The pot is a pencil rendering of one of her ceramic pots. Other pots using paper in 3-dimensions are by Miriam Kaye. Dorothy McGuinness builds her teapots with stiff strips of paper using a weaver's technique of plaiting. Holly Anne Mitchell builds with rolled up pages from comic books to result in a teapot built log-cabin style. Gugger Petter weaves with rolled up paper.

Gina Freuen, **Crow's Warning #3**. Multi media work on museum rag paper with pencil, collage, and computer scanned and printed media. 20" high, 16" wide, 1" deep. *Photo, artist*

If you think that Sean O'Meallie's teapots look like a take-off on a toy or other whimsical sculpture, you're right. Before O'Meallie began making sculptures, he was a toy designer. His pieces are usually termed playful or capricious, but each has a deeper meaning he tries to convey. He strives to entertain but at the same time engage the viewer to think and consider what he is trying to say. His shaping, assemblage, and painting are meticulous and brilliant in their sculptural quality, balance, and presentation.

So why does the wood worker make teapots?

More galleries are sponsoring teapot exhibitions and more private and museum collectors are seeking the unusual, thinking "teapot" instead of a vessel. Those who have been turning bowls and dishes for years are discovering there's a ready market for their work. Bin Pho, Michael Brolly, Jacques Vesery, and Alain Mailland, already enjoy gallery representation and loyal collectors. When del Mano Gallery director, Jan Peters, suggested they make teapots for an upcoming exhibit, Pho, Brolly, Vesery, and Mailland, virtuosos of their wood turning lathes, found that coming up with a variation on what they normally make by adding a spout, handle, and lid, was not a giant leap.

Alain Mailland's pieces were so organic and abstract that, with a little imagination and additional carving, he could evolve a piece with the necessary teapot elements. The result was a new direction for the wood artist, and an additional audience; now both teapot and wood art collectors.

Charles Cobb has been making teapots for some time along with a prodigious output of furniture and furnishings. For him, the teapot is a small, relaxing item to create that doesn't involve the machinations and tedious work of laminating, clamping, and finishing furniture. Delivery of teapots is a snap compared to delivering large tables, cabinets, and desks.

Michael Hosaluk, too, is well known for his wonderfully wild furniture that is often a take off on a plant. His cactus seats are an unexpected item for furniture and he carries the same humor and surprise into his teapots. His egg shaped head teapots with bright red lips and propeller tops are strictly fun, though the missing tooth on one of them mirrors the dental ordeal Hosaluk had just before making the pot. So there is something personal about it.

Edwin K. Hill's unusual use of cactus plants for the surfaces of his teapots reflect his lifelong search for unusual materials and innovative ways to use them. The *cholla* cactus family includes such plants as the stag horn, teddy bear, jumping cactus, and the walking stick, or cane. They are characterized by the overlapping sections of growth and have a wood inner skel-

Charles B. Cobb, **Teapot Container**. Maple, bleached and black dyed handle and top. The top has a gently chiseled texture. 14" high, 10" wide, 8" deep. *Photo, artist*

eton. When dried, the hollow structure is laminated to varying degrees of lenticular holes that provide a strong and light support for the plants growth. The patterns that result also make interesting different textures, and colors that lend themselves beautifully to a variety of teapot projects.

Hill's materials are as close as the desert floor near his Tucson, Arizona, home and studio. He says that "nature's design and architecture", as found in Arizona flora is merged with a free flowing, natural shape to become a teapot. He laminates small pieces of a cholla cactus over a removable core made of Styrofoam and covered with Fiberglas cloth saturated in resin. The wood segments and other materials are attached to the shell. Areas between pieces are filled in with a grout formed from resin and a filler material. The surface is sanded, the core is removed, leaving the hollow vessel. An oil finish rubbed into the wood is brought to a shiny finish with a paste wax.

Jackie Abrams' teapots are made of 100% cotton paper. She finds cotton paper made of 100% cotton fibers are superior in strength and durability to wood- pulp-based papers. Most papers in use for computer printing and any copying are wood pulp-based that often contain high concentrations of destructive acids. Cotton fiber papers, known to last several hundred years without fading, discoloration, or deteriorating, are most likely used for archival copies of important papers.

Cotton bond paper is available at most stationery and office product stores. For artwork, the paper should be white and measure 8.5 X 11". Cotton papers come in a variety of weights: 20, 24, or 28-lb. papers are most suitable and economical. After the paper is painted and varnished, it can be wiped off with a damp cloth.

Recycled paper is the medium for Holly Anne Mitchell. She likes the bright colors, typefaces, and interesting textures that she can achieve with rolled up pages from comics, foreign newspapers, the *Dow Jones Industrials* and *The Wall Street Journal*. It's the perfect marriage between creativity and ecology.

Gugger Petter has worked with newspaper as her main medium, creating both two and three-dimensional works for several years. Her large weavings are created from rolled newspaper tubes, which are then woven on hemp cord. The small teapot weavings employ the same technique. The papers are carefully selected to depict a simple, graphic, storytelling expression.

Certainly, trees and plants offer a variety of wonderful materials for teapot artists. They may tax and tickle one's imagination but that's what art is all about.

Donald E. Frith, **Teapot**. Porcelain, acrylic, and cherry wood. Combining contrasting materials results in a gutsy teapot with a sturdy unbreakable wood handle and top. 8.8" high, 7.25 wide, 4.25" deep. *Courtesy, del Mano Gallery, Los Angeles, California. Photo, David Peters©2004*

Sean O'Meallie, **Classic Argyle Light Bulb, Non-functional Wooden Teapot with Imitation Gold Finials**. 2003. Aspen, maple, cottonwood, birch, Krylon, and metal leaf. 16" high, 10.5" wide, 5.5" deep. *Courtesy, Mobilia Gallery, Cambridge, Massachusetts*

Sean O'Meallie, **Teapot On a Wheel**. 2002. Willow, teak, mahogany, Krylon, and steel. 22" high, 14" wide, 6.5" deep. *Collection, Gloria and Sonny Kamm. Courtesy, Mobilia Gallery, Cambridge, Massachusetts*

Binh Pho, **Tea for Two, I**. Poplar, acrylic, and gold leaf. 10" high, 9" wide, 6" deep. *Photo, artist*

Binh Pho, **Tea for Two, II** (open lid). *Photo, artist*

Binh Pho, **Tea for Two, II** (closed lid). 1995. Cherry wood, Amarillo, and bloodwood. 5" high, 9" wide, 6" deep. *Photo, artist*

Binh Pho, **Tea in Flight**. 2004. Maple burl and acrylic. 7.2" high, 8.75" wide, 4.4" deep. *Courtesy, del Mano Gallery, Los Angeles, California. Photo, David Peters©2004*

Binh Pho, **Tea in Flight** (detail). Pierced and painted surfaces. *Photo, artist*

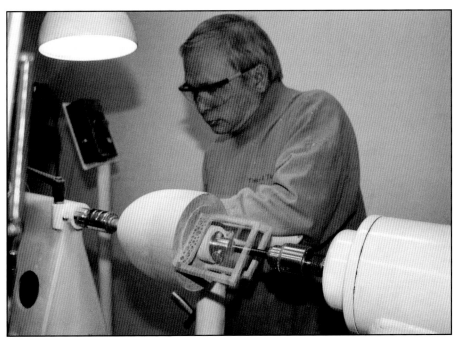

Binh Pho achieves the basic pot shape by turning the wood on a lathe.

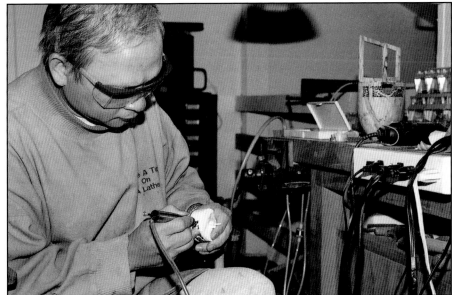

Perforations and other negative areas are shaped with a small hand drill.

197

Michael J. Brolly, **Yo! Tea Here**. 2004. Ash, dyed maple, and glass beads. Woodturning and construction. 7" high, 12" wide, 7.5" deep. Courtesy, *del Mano Gallery, Los Angeles, California. Photo, David Peters©2004*

Michael J. Brolly, **Tea for Two**. 2004. Ash and dyed maple. Wood turned and constructed. 9.5" high, 5.5" diam. *del Mano Gallery, Los Angeles, California. Photo, artist*

Michael Hosaluk, **Untitled Teapots**. 2003.
Maple, acrylic paint, and copper. 8" high, 4"
wide, 7" deep. *Photo, Grant Kernan*

Dona Z. Meilach, **Alphabet Tea**. Poplar. Constructed
wood cabinet and sawn letters assembled with a paper
printout of a Scrabble® board. Acrylic paint. The
cabinet door opens for storing the letters. 8" high, 8.5"
wide, 2" deep. *Photo,* artist

199

Jacques Vesery, **Tropical Breeze**. Carved and textured cherry, pear, ebony, and pigment. 4.25" high, 5.5" wide, 5.25" deep. *Collection, Gloria and Sonny Kamm. Courtesy, del Mano Gallery, Los Angeles, California. Photo, David Peters©2004*

Jacques Vesery, *Front:* **Escaping Your Inner Self**. Carved and textured cherry burl and box elder wood burl. 3" high, 4" wide, 5.75" deep. *Back:* **Amber Window to Enlightenment**. Carved and textured Swiss pear wood, amber, and 23k gold leaf. 6.75" high, 4.5" wide, 7" deep. *Collection, Gloria and Sonny Kamm. Courtesy, del Mano Gallery, Los Angeles, California. Photo, David Peters©2004*

Jacques Vesery, **Tame the Tension in My Clouds**. Cherry, Blackwood burl, and pigment. 5.75" high. 6.75" wide, 4.25" deep. *Courtesy, del Mano Gallery, Los Angeles, California. Photo, David Peters©2000*

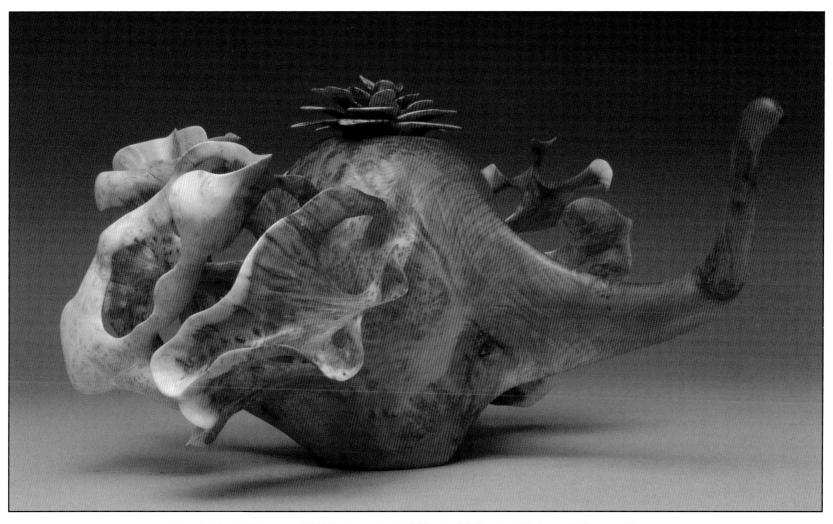

Alain Mailland, **Fantastea**! 2003. Juniper burl. 6.5" high, 13.3" wide, 10" deep. *Collection, Gloria and Sonny Kamm. Courtesy, del Mano Gallery, Los Angeles, California. Photo, David Peters©2004*

Constance Roberts, **Legali -Tea Set** (closed). 1999. Carved and painted wood. 11" high, 9" wide, 4" deep. *Collection, Gloria and Sonny Kamm. Photo, Tony Cunha*

Constance Roberts, **Legali -Tea Set** (open). *Photo, Tony Cunha*

Constance Roberts, **Adam and Eve Tea Set**. 1996. Carved and painted wood. Teapot:
7" high, 13" wide, 5.25" deep. Cup/saucer: 5.24" high, 6.75" wide, 5.5" deep. *Collection,
Gloria and Sonny Kamm. Photo, Tony Cunha*

David Sengel, **Untitled**. 1999. Australian grass tree wood, Jarrah wood, Hercules club thorns, blackberry thorns, and lacquer. 7.25" high, 10" wide, 6" deep. *Collection, Gloria and Sonny Kamm. Photo, Tony Cunha*

Tania Radda, **An Itsy-Bitsy, Please**. Painted basswood and maple, lathe-turned and hand carved. Insects, plants, and animals are her inspiration. This is a spider with a rounded shaped body; a smaller spider rests within. 10" high, 18" wide, 18" deep. *Photo, Tony Perez*

Charles B. Cobb, **Teapot Container**. Bleached maple with an African zebrawood handle. 14" high, 24" wide, 8" deep. *Photo, Hap Sakwa*

Charles B. Cobb, **Teapot Container**. Walnut, zebra, koa insert, maple drawers, and ball knobs painted copper. The knobs lift to reveal small drawers. 7" high, 7" wide, 5" deep. *Photo, Hap Sakwa*

Edwin K. Hill, **Cholla Tea**. Segments of wood from desert plants are laminated and illustrate the use of unusual materials. 9" high, 16" wide, 6" deep. *Photo, artist*

Edwin K. Hill, **Hard Hat Brew**. Strips of fir lumber and plywood are laminated over a Fiberglas shell. Steel parts are attached with screws, nails, and bolts. The wood is stained and sealed. Metal surfaces are also sealed to prevent oxidation. 18" high, 14" wide, 7" deep. *Photo, artist*

David French, **The Fabled Teapot**. 2001. Oil on carved wood. 8.5" high, 52" wide, 5.75" deep. *Collection, Gloria and Sonny Kamm. Photo, artist*

Jackie Abrams, **The Big Red Teapot**. Cotton paper, acrylic paint, waxed linen, and varnish. 13" high, 7" deep, 15" wide. *Collection, Jane and Steve Lorch. Mobilia Gallery, Cambridge. Massachusetts. Photo, Jeff Baird*

Jackie Abrams, **Tall, Tasty, and Tasteful**. Cotton paper, acrylic paint, waxed linen, and varnish. 12" high, 8" deep, 14" wide. *Mobilia Gallery, Cambridge. Massachusetts. Photo, Jeff Baird*

Dorothy McGuinness, **Grey Tweed**. Watercolor paper, acrylic paint, waxed linen, and ribbon. 8" high, 7.5" wide, 6.5" diam. *Photo, Jerry McCollum*

Dorothy McGuinness, **Tea For One**. Watercolor paper, acrylic paint, waxed linen, and ribbon. Techniques used are basket weaving starting with a spider weave, then working the body in a diagonal twill. 6.5" high, 5" wide, 2.5" diam. *Photo, Jerry McCollum*

Priscilla Henderson. **Tea Set**. 1997. Maple and rattan. The painted black maple overlays are a brilliant contrast for the woven natural rattan. 36" high, 17" wide, 17" deep. *Collection, Gloria and Sonny Kamm. Photo, Tony Cunha*

Margaret Wharton, **Mint Tea**. 1998. Cut up paperback book of the history of the U.S. Constitution. Epoxy, acrylic balls, photos of a book over a lake, cement, gold, and fake leaves. 12.5" high, 10" wide, 6.25" deep. *Collection, Gloria and Sonny Kamm. Photo, Tony Cunha*

Left:
Holly Anne Mitchell, **Teapot Sculpture**. Rolled Paper. Mitchell has elevated old newsprint to an exciting and inventive art medium. Assembly is in Lincoln Log fashion with gold-plaited beads. 4" high, 10" wide, 4.25" deep. *Collection, Gloria and Sonny Kamm. Photo, Tony Cunha*

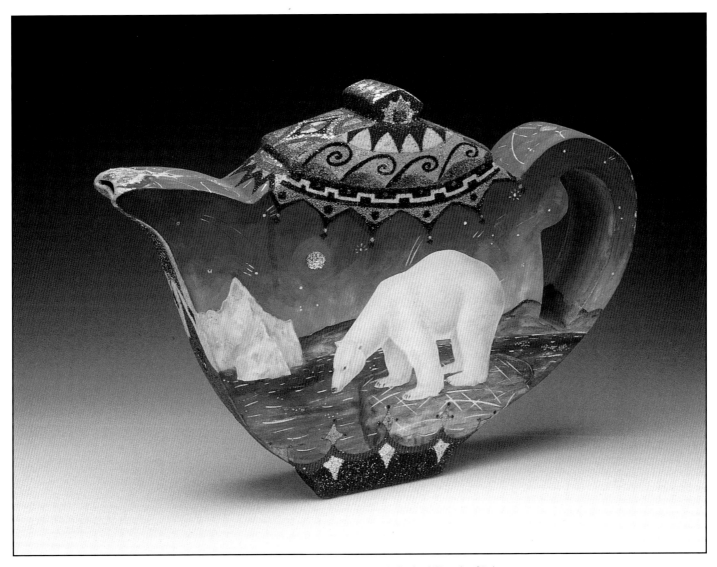

Miriam Kaye, **Soulstice**. 1994. Cardboard with plaster, paint, and glitter. 11" high, 15" wide, 3" deep.
Collection, Gloria and Sonny Kamm. Photo, Tony Cunha

Marjorie Schick, **Pour Vous**. 2003. Teapot with tray and detachable brooch. Painted wood, papier-mâché, and plastic laminate. Teapot: 14" high, 20.5" wide, 6" deep. Tray: 1.5" high, 18.5" diam. Brooch: 2" high, 4.1" diam. *Mobilia Gallery, Cambridge. Massachusetts. Photo, Gary Pollmiller*

Marjorie Schick, **Pour Vous Brooch** is the cover of the teapot made of painted wood with stainless steel wire. *Photo, Gary Pollmiller*

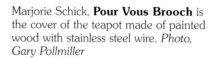

Gugger Petter, **Woman with Dog Teapot** (front and back views). Woven newspaper rolled into tubes that are then woven on hemp cord. The weavings are based on observations of daily life. Newspaper pages are carefully selected to depict a simple, graphic, and storytelling expression. 19.5" high, 21" wide, 6" deep. *Collection, Gloria and Sonny Kamm. Courtesy, Mobilia Gallery, Cambridge, Massachusetts.*

Gerda Rasmussen, **All Wrapped Up**. 2004. Gourd, fiber, beads, feathers, and cholla. The lid and spout are from a gourd; the handle is from a cholla cactus. Techniques are mainly wrapping, embroidery, and beading. 20" wide, 15" high, 12" deep. *Collection, Gloria and Sonny Kamm. Photo, Dona Meilach*

Chapter 9
Fibers, Fabrics, and Beads

Fibers, fabrics, beads, and their associated techniques, are contemporary materials for teapot makers. The materials are as unlikely for teapots as wood and paper and are also in the non-functional category.

Fiber artists may use sewing, quilting, basket coiling, knotting, wrapping, knitting, crocheting, plaiting, weaving, beading, and any combination of them. In addition to fibers and fabrics, they may use beads, plant parts, and gems. They may mix the techniques to help them manipulate around a form and add textural interest to a piece. Fiber teapots show remarkable flamboyance as well as restraint. The successful teapots meld technique with color, design, form, and structure.

Gerda Rasmussan's skill with wrapping is evident in her *All Wrapped Up* fiber teapot sculpture. Tight wrapping, coiling, and twisting give the shape a rigidity. She has added shells and beads. The spout and lid are pieces cut from a large gourd and painted. The handle is a piece of cholla cactus found in the dessert. She has perched a saucy can-can doll, also made by wrapping, sewing, and beading, near the handle. The doll has a beaded tiara embellished with feathers. Gerda Rasmussen made her teapot specifically for this book. It was sold immediately when Sonny Kamm saw it in my studio waiting to be photographed. He said it was an "over the top" expression for a teapot.

Joanne Russo's Red Button Teapot begins with the black ash basket, and then beads, buttons, and plastic tubing are sewn on. The construction is an "additive" process similar to collage. Irene C. Reed's pieces are also additive in that they "grow" by building up forms with yarn as she crochets.

Words formed from tiny beads are not an easy task. Beading words are worked in a similar manner as the patterns made with tiny seed beads by Native Americas for their moccasins, jackets, neckwear, and other adornments. It's a time-consuming labor of love process. All fiber artists seem to have an abundance of patience, requiring hundreds of hours, days, weeks, and often months to fashion one or two objects.

The teapot offers a new challenge to fiber artists and they are rising to meet it and beat it. Collectors quickly have subscribed to this soft sculpture scene as they seek fresh and refreshing ideas.

Gerda Rasmussen, **All Wrapped Up**. Detail showing can-can girl and intricacies of the wrapping. *Photo, Dona Meilach*

Merrill Morrison, **Iced Tea**. Waxed linen, glass seed beads, and glass bugle beads. 6.25" high, 9.25" wide, 5.75" deep. *Courtesy, del Mano Gallery, Los Angeles, California. Photo, David Peters©2004*

Jeanette Ahlgren, **Piccolé Takes a Break**. 1997. Glass seed beads woven with stainless steel wire and appliquéd with polyester. 10" high, 9" wide, 7" deep. *Collection, Gloria and Sonny Kamm. Mobilia Gallery, Cambridge, Massachusetts. Photo, Tony Cunha*

Candace Kling, **At Your Service**. 2002. Acetate satin fabric, nylon thread, copper rod, lightweight buckram, and glues. Techniques include molding, folding, pressing, stitching, and gluing. Kling created this piece with a nod to the bow tied, starch shirted 1950s gas station attendant. 12" high, 10.5" wide, 4" deep. *Courtesy, Mobilia Gallery, Cambridge, Massachusetts. Photo, John Bagley*

Irene C. Reed, **Carmen Miranda Teapot**. 2004. A purse made of crocheted cotton, metallic threads, trapunto quilting, fabric, and beads. 10" high, 9" wide, 4.2" deep. *Courtesy, del Mano Gallery, Los Angeles, California. Photo, David Peters©2004*

Irene C. Reed, **Flamingo Tea**. 2004. Purse made of crocheted cotton, metallic thread, trapunto quilting and fabric. The purse separates from the base that serves as a display stand, and as the flamingo's legs and feet. 14.2" high, 9.5" wide, 7.5" deep. *Collection, Gloria and Sonny Kamm. Courtesy, del Mano Gallery, Los Angeles, California. Photo, David Peters©2004*

Irene C. Reed. Stand for **Flamingo Tea**, with the purse beside it. *Photo, David Peters©2004*

219

Kate Anderson, **Jim Dine and Frank Stella**. Teapots of knotted waxed linen and stainless steel. Each: 10.75" high, 7" wide, 2.5" deep. *Courtesy, Snyderman/Works Gallery, Philadelphia, Pennsylvania. Photo, Tony Deck*

Angie Harbin, **Jacque's Teapot**. Nylon, epoxy resin, paint and threads. 10.25" high, 15" wide, 6.3" deep.
Courtesy, del Mano Gallery, Los Angeles, California. Photo, David Peters©2004

Sarah Crawford, **Tea Cosy**. Latex sheet layered, punch, pleated, and woven through with elastic fishing line. Sized to fit a small "Brown Betty" teapot. *Courtesy, Mobilia Gallery, Cambridge, Massachusetts. Photo, Richard Stroud*

Thomas H. Wegman. **Untitled**. Front and back views. 1999. Beaded and jeweled found teapot. Beadwork takes its cue for Indian moccasins. Hours of painstakingly detailed work were required to place each bead in the design desired 8" high, 10.25" wide, 5.5" deep. *Collection, Gloria and Sonny Kamm. Photo, Tony Cunha*

JoAnne Russo, **Red Button Teapot**. 2004. Black ash basket with, cactus spines, plastic tubing, pine needles, and beads. The baskets are woven and the beads and cactus spines are sewn on. 13" high, 9" wide, 7" deep. *Photo, Jeff Baird*

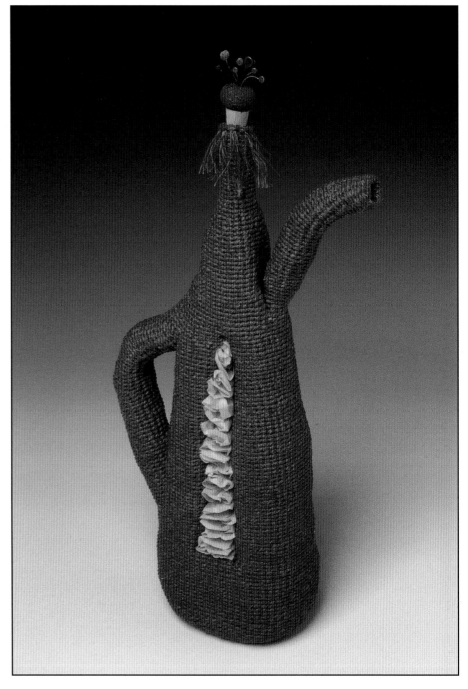

Michael and Michelle Lalonde, **Tea Time Teapot**. Silk screened lamb suede, stitched together, beaded, and formed over the teapot base. The handle is made of beads on wire. The spout is beaded with seed beads. The lid lifts off revealing a small compartment. It was created for a museum show and sold immediately. *Photo, Jeff Baird*

Right:
Mary Hettmansperger, **Tea for Polly**. Waxed linen twined. A fiber teapot made to provide help and emotional support for a friend through a healing process. 18.5" high, 6" wide, 4" deep. *Photo Jeff Baird*

Marilyn Moore, **Green Tea**. 2002. Fiber technique of twining but using stitched copper wire cloth with copper wire. 10" high, 10" wide, 5.5" deep. *Photo, Jerry McCollum*

Marilyn Moore, **Aladdin's Teapot**. 1999. Fabric technique of twining with magnet wire over copper wire, with glass beads. 4.5" high, 8" wide, 6" deep. *Photo, Jerry McCollum*

Axel Russmeyer, **Teapot**. Dazzling beadwork and sumptuous color are the hallmarks of Axel Russmeyer's work. 10" high, 8" wide, 5" deep. *Courtesy, Mobilia Gallery, Cambridge, Massachusetts.*

Reina Mia Brill, **Flight of Enchantment**. Teapot with stand and base. Hand-knit coated copper wire, brass, and wood. 12" high, 8" wide, 6" deep. *Photo, artist*

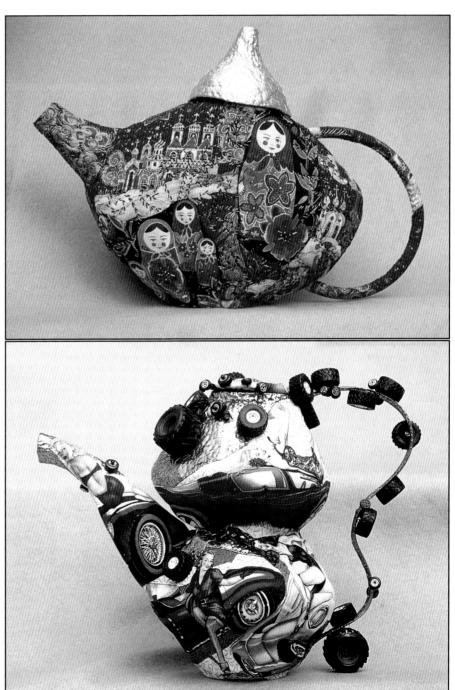

Above:
Mary Beth Bellah, **Suits Me To A Tea**. Wool suiting, cotton shirting, silk ties, buckram, boning, copper mesh, cotton batting, hand-formed base, appliquéd and quilted. 12.5" high, 15" wide, 6" deep. *Photo, artist*

Top right:
Mary Beth Bellah, **Russian Caravan Tea**. Commercial cotton, buckram, boning, copper mesh, tubing, cotton batting, hand-formed base, appliquéd quilted and beaded. 10" high, 15.5" wide, 5" deep. *Photo, artist*

Right:
Mary Beth Bellah, **Fast Lane Tea-sers**! Commercial cottons, buckram, boning, copper mesh, cotton batting, wheels, hand-formed base, appliquéd, quilted, and embellished. 12" high, 15" wide, 8" deep. *Snyderman/Works Gallery, Philadelphia, Pennsylvania. Photo, artist*

Yuyen Chang, **Teabag Teapot**.
2003. Actual unwrapped, gently
used teabags, string, and packaged
teabags. 5.5" high, 3.5" wide, 5"
deep. *Collection, Gloria and Sonny
Kamm. Photo, Tom McInvaille*

JoAnne Russo, **Cactus Tea Pot**. Black ash, cactus spines, plastic tubing, pine needles, and beads. 9" high, 11" wide, 10" deep. *Photo, Jeff Baird*

Linda Hansen Mau, **Paper Clay Teapot**. Porcelain paper clay over a steel wire base. The paper clay is covered with red terra sigillata, (a type of clay slip), electric fired to cone 04, and smoked in an open washtub with newspaper. 7" high, 11" wide, 6" deep. *Photo, artist*

Chapter 10

Tea Potpourri

When teapot artists run out of materials familiar to them, what are they to do? Look for something else with which to capture their visions. Alternatively, if someone is deeply into another medium and wants to make teapots, they have to think out of the pot, so to speak, and evolve a solution that will satisfy their creative yens.

That's what you will find in this chapter. A few of the just-happen-to-work pieces in out-of-the-ordinary media are by art students and suggest promising careers for them. They find an inventive use for something ordinary in an extraordinary way.

Among the materials you will discover in this chapter are *paper clay* and *polymer clay*. Both products can be explored in greater depth at several Web sites that can be found in an Internet search. They are also advertised in craft publications.

Paper Clay

"Paper clay" is a non-toxic modeling material that can be sculpted, molded, or shaped and air dried (no baking!) to a hard finish that can be carved or sanded. The product can be purchased ready for mixing but Linda Hansen Mau has learned to make her own. She merges three of her ongoing interests; a love of teapots, a curiosity about materials and how to manipulate them in new ways, and the role of "function" in ceramic art. In her series of non-functioning vessels, the pieces are first fabricated in steel wire then coated with her own formula for paper clay. Says Mau, "New materials often demand new techniques and lead to new solutions to old design problems Using paper clay combined with steel wire has opened up a new area of design exploration."

Other materials you will discover in the teapots in this chapter are sturgeon skin, by Jan Hopkins, rubber investment bowls by Julie Luckenill, Lego blocks by Joel Nishimura, matches in Styrofoam by Michelle Hallacy, and many more.

There is no end to the inventiveness of the creative mind that, indeed, creates a tea potpourri.

Linda Hansen Mau, **Paper Clay Teapot**. Porcelain paper clay over a steel wire base. The paper clay is covered with red terra sigillata, (a type of clay slip), electric fired to cone 04, and smoked in an open washtub with newspaper. 16" high, 20" wide, 8" deep. *Photo, artist*

Polymer Clay

"Polymer clay" is a pliable (blend-able) polymer compound for artists and crafters. It's not a true clay; clay is fine particles of silicate suspended in water, whereas polymer clay is fine particles of polyvinyl chloride (PVC) suspended in a plasticizer —but its characteristics and handling are clay-like.

What makes polymer clay special is its versatility. It comes in dozens of colors that can be blended like paints to make new colors. Since the color is inherent in the particles, two or more colors can be worked together without blending them. It enables the artists to create special effects such as cane work and marbling. The clay's pliability and ductility lend themselves to the same techniques one might use for glasswork, textile arts, and sculpture. Polymer clay doesn't dry out, so you can sculpt and form it without worrying about a time limit. It is hardened by baking in a home oven.

Wayne S. Sutton, **Honey Box.** 1997. Found objects constructed. 8.5" high, 6" wide, 3.5" deep. *Photo, artist*

Michelle Hallacy, **TeaHot**.
Detail of body and handle.
Photo, Gary Pollmiller

Michelle Hallacy, **TeaHot**. Teapot of matches and constructed rubberized foam. 10.5" high, 12" wide, 21" deep.
Photo, Gary Pollmiller

Bill Colligen's Gourd Teapots

Bill Colligen finds gourds a unique vehicle for teapots. Traditionally, gourds, believed to have originated in Africa, have been used for thousands of years as a food and water-storing vessel. They are still a valued necessity used by many tribes throughout the world.

Colligen enhances this natural material with a variety of designs and exciting, original embellishments. As a canvas, and a material that can be shaped into a teapot, it has exquisite qualifications. But gourds don't happen overnight. Their growing and drying processes can take up to an entire year for larger specimens. Many natural patterns caused by moisture from inside appear on the gourd's shells. Once dried they are resilient, can be worked like wood, and can last a lifetime.

Pyro-engraving tools are used for engraving some of the designs into the gourd. They yield a charred or burned color contrast. Colligen may also use diamond and carbide bits for carving. Many of his pieces are colored with atomized metal powders mixed into an acrylic medium and then applied in several layers to the surface. He then uses an oxidation process to create colored patinas. Embellishments may include precious stones, reeds, bamboo root, and products of nature. His designs and detailing are inspired by old Raku pottery from Japan, modern pieces from Asian cultures, and Native American pottery patterns.

It took some time for Bill Colligen to find a type of gourd that adapted itself perfectly to a teapot by cutting off the neck and using it for the spout. When rejoined and finished no seam can be detected. Colorants are a mixture of metal powders (brass, copper, iron, or bronze) in a matte acrylic medium. Additional oxidizing agents and dyes are mixed to create the unique patinas. The entire process takes 3-4 days. Images are carved with dental burrs and an X-Acto knife.

Bill Colligen, **Gourd Teapot**. Gourd with a Chinese coin on a brown jade knob, a band of gold leaf, and a rattan handle. All dots are applied one at a time with acrylic paint, around the shoulder of the pot that has a metallic green patina finish. 4.5" high. *Photo, George Post*

Bill Colligen carves the lid for a gourd teapot. *Photo, Ron Frederick*

Bill Colligen, **Gourd Teapot**. Gourd with a brass knob topped by a Chinese coin. Two bands are inset for color and texture. The top one is Japanese silver leaf, and a bottom band is dyed to simulate burl wood (faux burl?). *Photos, artist*

Bill Colligen's gourd teapot assembly line will become the canvases and sculptural form for Colligen's non-functional teapots. Though each gourd teapot has a unique design, several bases are prepared at one time. The cut off gourd neck is cut down and inserted into the space where it had been attached. An epoxy is used to adhere the spout to each gourd, it is then sanded, smoothed, painted, embellished, and the handle is attached.

Hap Sakwa, **Mad Hatter's Teapot**. Mosaic collage and found objects. Dice and marbles are used for the feet. The cap is the crown from a liquor bottle with a coin as the finial. 9" high, 11" wide, 9" deep. *Photo, artist*

Julie Luckenbill, **Investment Teapot**. 2004. An exploration into the use of rubber and nickel. The body is made of two rubber investment bowls used by dentists to mix plaster. A repeat functional and decorative element is the rubber cord used to sew the parts together. The top is nickel. 10" high, 7.5" wide, 7" deep. *Photo, artist*

Jan Hopkins, **Sturgeon General's Teapot**. 1998. Sturgeon skin and waxed linen. 9" high, 10" wide, 5" deep. *Collection, Sonny and Gloria Kamm. Photo, Tony Cunha*

Joel Nishimura, **Lego Teapot**. The popular toy building blocks make a unique teapot. The piece is one of a series depicting "The Nature of Things." 3.5" high, 6" wide, 3" deep. *Photo, Roger Schreiber*

Linda Mau, **Paper Clay Teapot**. Paper clay can provide a valid medium for making nonfunctional teapots. It is easy to shape and pierce before it hardens. 8.5" high, 8.5" wide, 6" deep. *Photo, artist*

Gail Rappa lives in a turn-of-the-century historic town surrounded by reminders of the past. As a result, the objects she finds to inspire her teapots are special because of the mystery and history they represent. The humble form of alchemy that occurs when a common material is combined with silver and gold, turns it into something precious that intrigues her. This is evident in her *Tea For One* that is tiny in size but monumental in design and the impact it makes on a viewer.

Gail Rappa, **Tea for One**. 2002. Tea set of river stones, sterling silver, 14k gold, fossilized coral, and a moonstone. As an avid tea drinker, Rappa likes the ritual involved in brewing and drinking tea. The piece is a tribute to a solitary cup of tea. There is a secret fortune inside the pot…her version of reading tea leaves. Teapot: 3" high, 4" wide. *Collection, Walter Cuchine. Photo, Hap Sakwa*

Blanka Šperková, **Knitted Teapot
with Stand and Spoon**. Wire. The
handle and spout are one piece that
runs through the teapot. *Inset*: The
teapot rests on the dish-like stand and
the spoon slides into the spout.
*Courtesy, Mobilia Gallery, Cambridge,
Massachusetts.*

Steven Goldate, **A Virtual Teapot**. 2000. Computer-generated image of a futuristic teapot. A set of four different perspectives rendered in stereo was incorporated into a sculpture of the same title. *Inset:* The "peep box," through which four different computer-generated images of **A Virtual Teapot** can be viewed. Another one is in the Queensland University of Technology Art Collection, Queensland, Australia. *Collection, Gloria and Sonny Kamm. Courtesy, artist*

Brian Peshek, **It's a Cold World T-Pot**. Found objects; a glove, ceramic faucet knob, tin funnel, and a hand made wood key. 20" high. *Collection, Gloria and Sonny Kamm. Photo, artist*

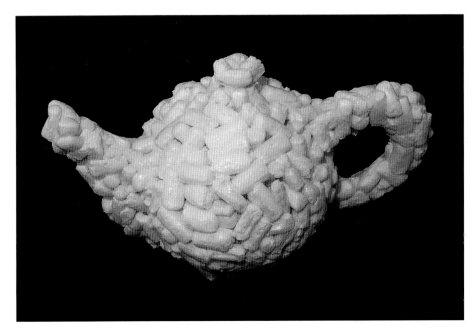

Brian Peshek, **Excelsior T-Pot**. Biodegradable starch peanut shaped packing material used to secure items during shipping. The idea is to make a precious item (teapot) from un-precious materials. It represents a play on the purpose of materials; a contradiction of roles. 9" high. *Photo, artist*

Carole Beadle, **Red Hot Teapot.** Electronic aluminum wire manipulated and woven. 18" high, 14" wide, 3" deep. *Mobilia Gallery, Cambridge, Massachusetts. Photo, artist*

Brian Peshek, **Candle-wax Teapot**. A mold was built to use for casting the wax. 6" high. *Photo, artist*

Leslie Tiano, **A Round of Tea**. Copper, acrylic, silver, die-form, and etching. 5" diam., 1.5" deep. *Photo, Helen Shirk*

Right:
Ron Baron, **Home Sweet Home**. 2002. Pennies, glue, wood, and bronzed baby shoes. The pennies are layered, tier upon tier, much like a bricklayer. "I have only created these works periodically; inspired during moments when I have been drawn to repetition as a means for solace and self-reflection." 24" high, 18" wide, 10" deep. *Collection, Gloria and Sonny Kamm. Photo, artist*

Cynthia Toops, a jeweler who has explored polymer clay in depth, has turned the material into jewelry shaped as teapots.

Dawn Emms, **Dream Brewers Infusion Pot**. 2000. Brooch. Cellulose, acetate, and silver. 4.75" high, 3" wide. *British Crafts Council. Courtesy, Jen Haybach, SOFA Chicago, Illinois*

Cynthia Toops, **Beneath the Big Top**. Pendant of polymer clay micro-mosaic and sterling silver. 3" high. *Mobilia Gallery, Cambridge, Massachusetts. Photo, Dan Adams*

Joan Irvin, **Tea for Two**. China paint, enamel, copper, sterling silver, with pearls, lapis, and silk. 1" high, 1.5" domes, 16" neck loop. *Photo, artist*

245

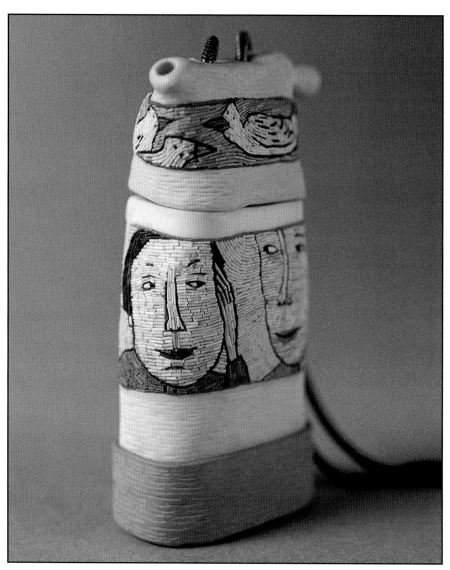

Cynthia Toops, **Untitled**. 1999. Polymer clay micro-mosaic teapot. 3.5" high. *Photo, Dan Adams*

Cynthia Toops, **Untitled**. Reverse side. Note that the cups shown are contained in the lower compartment. *Photo, Dan Adams*

Laura Balombini, **Untitled Teapot**. Polymer
clay and steel wire. 10.5" high, 8" wide, 6" deep.
*Courtesy, del Mano Gallery. Photo, David
Peters©2004*

Selected Bibliography

Adamson, Glenn and Davira S. Taragin. *Tea, Anyone? The Donna Moog Teapot Collection.* Racine Art Museum, Wisconsin: Racine Art Museum, 2003.

Carter, Tina M. *Collectible Teapots: A Reference and Price Guide.* Iola, Wisconsin. Krause Publications, 2000.

Chavarria, Joaquim. *The Big Book of Ceramics.* New York, New York: Watson-Guptill Publications, 1994.

Clark, Garth. *American Ceramics.* 1876 to the Present. New York, New York: Abbeville Press, 1986.

Clark, Garth. *The Eccentric Teapot, Four Hundred Years of Invention.* New York, New York: Abbeville Press, 1989.

Clark, Garth. *The Artful Teapot.* New York, New York: Watson-Guptill Publications, 2001.

Editors, *500 Teapots.* Asheville, North Carolina: Lark Books, 2002.

Ellis, William S. *Glass.* New York, New York: Avon Books, Inc., 1998.

Ferrin, Leslie. *Teapots Transformed.* Madison, Wisconsin: Guild Publishing, 2000.

Ketchum, Jr. William C. and others. *American Ceramics, Collection of Everson Museum of Art.* New York, New York: Rizzoli International Publications, Inc., 1989.

Levin, Elaine. *The History of American Ceramics, 1907 to the Present.* New York, New York: Harry N. Abrams, Inc., 1988.

Peterson, Susan. *The Craft and Art of Clay.* New York, New York: Overlook Press; 2nd edition. 1996

Richerson, David W., *The Magic of Ceramics.* Westerville, Ohio: The American Ceramics Society: 2000.

Rosen Diana. *Taking Time for Tea.* Storey Books. Pownal, Vermont: 2000.

Sandon, Henry. *Coffee Pots and Teapots for the Collector.* New York, New York: Arco Publishing Co., Inc., 1974.

Savage, George and Harold Newman. *An Illustrated Dictionary of Ceramics.* London, England & New York, New York: Thames & Hudson Ltd., 2000.

SOFA Exhibition Catalogs. Expression of Culture Inc., Chicago, Illinois. 2001-2004.

Tichane, Robert. *Ash Glazes.* Iola, Wisconsin: Krause Publications 1998.

Tippett, Paul. *Teapots- Christie's Collectibles.* Canada: Little, Brown and Company, Ltd., 1996.

Resources

There is more information available on the Internet than can possibly be listed here.
Search for:
Antiques
Ceramic teapots
Collectibles
Contemporary teapots
Teapot collectors
Teapots
Teapot exhibits
Teapots, museums
Names of all the galleries listed in the acknowledgments

Art and Craft publications:
American Craft
American Style
Metalsmith
Ceramics Monthly
Ceramic Art and Perception
Glass

Index